The Dvořá
For Czech and,

OCCASIONAL P⌐⌐⌐.⌐. ....
No.7

Traces in the Sand:
The Story of Anthony Kammel
in 18th Century Britain

by

Sylva Šimsová

**Dedicated to Zdeňka Pilková,
who enriched my life
by introducing me to Anthony Kammel**

Newcastle-under-Lyme: The Dvořák Society

The Dvořák Society is a Registered Charity No. 267336

Published by

The Dvořák Society
For Czech and Slovak Music

This Edition
First Published: 2014

ISBN 978-0-9562608-0-2
(Soft covers)

ISBN 978-0-9562608-1-9
(Hard bound)

Printed by:
Greenhouse Graphics
Bramley
Hampshire
RG26 5DL

The Dvořák Society is grateful to the Czech Ministry of Foreign Affairs Department of Cultural Affairs for Czechs Living Abroad (MZV-OKKV) for financial assistance with the production of its various publications

CONTENTS

Cover Illustration:

Frontispiece of Opus 4 as published by Welcker of London

4

PREFACE

Musicologists are always happy when able to discover unknown compositions or bring forgotten personalities to the public's notice. Such activities are quite adventurous at times – documents are discovered which can often be several centuries old, in many cases it is necessary to subject sources to critical evaluation, and even contemporary literature puts controversial explanations on events at times. Getting names of authors mixed up is no rarity. Such is the case of Antonín Kammel, some of whose works have been attributed to Haydn.

Zdeňka Pilková (1931–1999) devoted almost all her life to the music of the 18th century. Her first book was a study of the melodramas and singspiels of Jiří Antonín Benda (publ. 1960). She also wrote an extensive book on the musicians from the Czech Lands at the Dresden Court in the 18th century (still in MS) and a study of Jan Jiří Neruda (1711–1776) published in the Beiträge zur Musikgeschichte Ostmittel, Ost- und Südosteuropas (Edition IME 1999) which includes a thematic catalogue of that composer's works (pp.103-150). Zdeňka Pilková gave dozens of papers, wrote a large number of reviews and many exhibition catalogues and lectured in various countries, including the USA.

She took an interest in Antonín Kammel quite early on, writing a paper on him for a Haydn conference in Washington in 1975 (publ. 1981). Then in collaboration with Sylva Šimsová she wrote about Kammel's Will (1993, 1995-96) and together they continued to uncover much new information about him. Her untimely death put paid to the completion of her various projects.

Jiří Pilka

INTRODUCTION

When some years ago my late friend, Zdeňka Pilková, was writing her *New Grove* entry on Anthony Kammel, she asked me to find out whether during his time in London he had any children, as she herself was not allowed to travel to London at the time. I visited the church of St George in Hannover square and extracted for her the names of Kammel's children from the register of births.

This led to my own research into Anthony Kammel, not just his musical activities, but also his life as a newcomer to Britain and I kept collecting material about him and his social life.

When post-1989 Zdeňka Pilková and I were able to meet again, we started planning a book about Anthony Kammel, combining her view as a musicologist and my own as a social historian.

Unfortunately, Zdeňka Pilková's part of the book was never completed because of her untimely death. I am therefore presenting my own part which deals with the life of a Central European musician who contributed to British musical life in the 18th century and whose descendants are living among us today.

Sylva Šimsová

ACKNOWLEDGEMENTS

I would to thank the following:

The Dvořák Society for Czech and Slovak Music, especially Graham Melville-Mason and Shawn Pullman for their encouragement and help. My son Cyril Šimsa who helped me to collect some of the data and found Anthony Kammel's Will.
My husband Karel Janovický who edited the text.
Jiří Pilka who made it possible for me to access Zdeňka's research papers after her death.

Most of all I am grateful to Zdeňka Pilková herself for introducing me to Anthony Kammel.

Sylva Šimsová

TRACES IN THE SAND:

The Story of Anthony Kammel
in 18th Century Britain

His feelings are often as tender as those of Pugnani and as delicate as those of Philidor and always as beautiful and true as those of Abel. He is aware of the nature and limitations of his instruments and is able to use this knowledge to the best advantage of musical truth. Kammel understands how to blend colours and to contrast light and shade, his melodies are beautiful and his harmony excellent. His style is full, rounded and compact – and yet always transparent.

CHAPTER I

ANTE

Migration of musicians from the Czech Lands

Migration of musicians from the Lands of the Czech Crown during the middle and second half of the eighteenth century was high. Active musical culture and education gave rise to relatively high numbers of musicians while prospects of finding a job abroad were good. According to the Dlabač Lexikon, 409 of 951 people who at the beginning of the 19th century cited music as their main occupation lived abroad.[1]

Zdeňka Pilková in her paper on "Music in Bohemia 1740-1810"[2] says that some of the Czech musicians at foreign chateaus and other places formed little expatriate colonies - founded by the first successful migrants, they soon grew by attracting others.

The same is true – though to a lesser extent - about musicians from Central Europe in London during the period. The life of Anthony Kammel is a good example of one such migrant.

Although he is spoken of as a Czech musician, he spoke Czech, German, Italian and English. In a letter to Count Vincent Waldstein he claimed: "...I have done German and Bohemian virtuosity so much honour, as nobody else here in England was able to do...".[3]

Kammel acquired English as his fourth language, after the language of Italy where he had studied. He married an English wife and his children were probably brought up speaking only English.

What did Kammel do before coming to London?

Antonín (also Anthony) Kammel (also Kammell, Kamel, Kamml, Cammell, Cammel) was baptized on 21 April 1730 in Bělec on the Waldstein estate where his father Jan Jiří Kammel was an estates forester. His mother's name was Maří Magdalena. He had a younger

---

[1] Dlabač, Jan Bohumír. (1815)
[2] Pilková, Zdeňka: *Music in Bohemia 1740-1810: The Historical and Social Scene and Its Changes.* Typescript in private ownership.
[3] Freemanová, Michaela & Mikanová, Eva (2003b) p.216

sister baptised Anna Magdalena on 28 July 1732.[4]

From 1746 to 1751 Anthony Kammel studied at the Patres Piares Grammar School in Slaný, 25km NW of Prague where he also received the thorough musical education that was customary at Piarist schools in those days.

He went to university in Prague, studying philosophy from 1751 to 1753. For the year 1753-54 he was entered as studying at the faculty of law which required two years of philosophy as a precondition. His Professor there was Josephus Daniel De Waldt.[5]

But it was his musical talent that finally decided his career.

His patron Count Vincent of Waldstein paid for his journey to Italy where he studied with Giuseppe Tartini in Padua.[6] Tartini himself had between 1723 and 1726 been a student of the Czech composer and organist Bohuslav Matěj Černohorský, known during his four visits to Italy as Padre Boemo.[7]

---

[4] In the manuscripts of Zdeňka Pilková there is the following note about Kammel's baptism being recorded on a loose sheet inserted into the register of baptisms, probably in 1732: "Matrika narozených – fara Zbečno, kraj Rakovník, od 1725-1742 SA Praha 2 Karlov, Horská 7. [sinature] Zbečno M2 21-17 sv.3 folio 57 vložka. Mezi str 56 a 57 vložen listek psaný nikoliv farářem Georgiem Horákem, ale rukou J.Leopolda Losa, který psal matriku až od února 1732. Text tohoto volně vloženého lístku (kurentem): "Anno Z Bielcze 1730.Dne 21.Aprilis pokřztieny gest Syn Johann Anton z pocztiwych Rodiczuw otce Jana Jiržika Kammla ten czas fořssta Bieleszkyho a Materže Maryi Magdaleny. Podd: Kržiwoklatsky. Levans. Wzacztny Pan Augustin Roth (feldster?) Kržiwolatsky, Testes. Wzacztny Pan Balthasar Breinnholiter obroczny Nyžbersky? A Pani Dorota Manzielka Pana Ferdinanda Skyziny Polesnyho Kržiwoklatskyho. Per me curatum J. Lepoldum"; [dale záznam v téže matrice str.80]. "28.Julia 1732 pokřtěna jest dcera jmenem Anna Magdalena z poctivých rodiču otce Jana Khamia [sic] a Mateře Magdaleny. Podd. Křiwoklatsky. Levans. Dorota Manzielka Jana Ferdinanda Skyziny z Bielče."

[5] Archiv UK M11 Rectores, decani, professores omnium facultatum 1654-1776: From 1754 in "Professores iuris" for the subject "Insitutionum" prof. Josephus Daniel Dewald who later lectured on canonical law.
Archiv Uk M33 In a folder for 1764 there is a double page [dvoulist] with the names of de Waldt's students for 1753-54 "Nomina DD Auditorum qui Ao 1753 et respective 1754 frequentant apud Professorem De Waldt. Kammel is registered as "D.Antonio Kammel Boh. bieleczeusensis"

[6] Vincent Valdštejn 1731-1797; Archiv Valdštejnský in SA Mnichovo Hradiště: Corr.V.V. 1755-1791; corr. of the accountant Kochlitz 1741-1753; accounts V.V. 1760-1799; Misc. V.V. 1747-1845

[7] Petrobelli, Pierluigi. *Giuseppe Tartini. Le fonti biografiche*. Venezia, 1968 (Studi di musica veneta. no.1.)

On his return from Italy, Kammel gave concerts in Prague. He was said to dazzle his audiences with his cantilena in slow movements. In spite of his success, he disappeared from Prague sometime during the winter 1764-5 and was later heard of in London. The reasons for his departure are not known. Dlabač speculated that Kammel's reason for leaving Prague was a woman.[8] This is possible, as according to more than one of his letters he enjoyed the admiration of women: "...When I play the adagio one could hear the ladies sigh...".[9]

His fortunes since leaving Prague and until March 1765 remain a mystery. He fairly quickly moved through Germany and the Netherlands, earning a living most likely by playing the violin while on his way. On arrival in London, he wrote in one of his letters to Count Vincent Waldstein that he "still had 130 golden ducats which he had earned in Würzburg and Rotterdam".[10]

His first stop in Germany was probably in Bavaria. The programmatic titles of some movements of his symphonies from that period seem to point in that direction: "Allegro representa Buergheim-Pfaltz", "Adagio representa Auerhann-Pfaltz". In February 1765, he sent a letter to his sponsor Count Vincent Waldstein from Regensburg. The Pfaltz in these titles clearly referring to Oberpfalz in Bavaria. What motivated him to mention these places in his composition? Was it love or money? (Composers at the time expected to be rewarded by their dedicatees.) Or did he make new friends there? Did his future brother-in-law Charles Christian Besser live there?[11]

He also informed Count Waldstein that he was planning to travel through Würzburg to Mannheim, reporting in his next letter the stormy crossing

---

[8] Fetis, Francois Joseph (1898) v.4 p.472 says "Tout a coup, il disparut de cette ville sans qu'on sut se qu'il etai devenu; ce ne fut qu'apres un certain temps qu'on apparit qu'il etait a Londres"; Dlabač, Jan Bohumír (1815) v.2.p.38 says "...und soll eine reiche Dame, da er eine andere zuvor in Bohmen nich erhalten konnte, und wegen ihr auch sein Vaterland zu verlassen gezwungen wurde, zur Ehe erhalten haben".

[9] Freemanová, Michaela & Mikanová, Eva (2003b) p.215

[10] Freemanová, Michaela & Mikanová, Eva (2003b) p.212

[11] Only two compositions dating from the first half of the sixties, during Kammel's supposed stay in Pfalz are known. But it can be assumed, in view of the custom of the time, that there were more of these sinfonias, at least three, possibly six. The first is Sinfonia in G, published in a modern edition edited by Zdeňka Pilková, is based on the sole available source, the transcript of parts preserved in the Rajhrad Monastery of the Augustinians in Moravia. The title page of the transcript is dated 1766 and Father Alexius is named as the author of the transcript. The other known Sinfonia from the "Pfalz" series [in D] was not preserved in Rajhrad, but in Bakov in Bohemia, transcribed in the 1760s by the teacher Augustine Fibiger.

he had from Rotterdam to England.[12]

The reason for his coming to England remains obscure. He was a young talented musician with not much money and probably with a sense of adventure. The success German musicians were having in London may have spurred him on. He also may have known some Englishmen, such as Horace Mann, whom he had met during his stay in Italy.

---

[12] Freemanová, Michaela & Mikanová, Eva (2003b) p.212

16

CHAPTER II

KAMMEL'S LIFE IN BRITAIN

KAMMEL'S LIFE IN BRITAIN

Kammel and the musical life in Britain

Kammel's arrival in London

According to his letter to Count Vincent Waldstein, Kammel arrived in London on 29 March 1765.[1] Leopold Mozart's travel notes for that year confirm that he met Kammel during his visit to London.[2]

In London Kammel earned money by playing at concerts: either in the orchestra, or leading the orchestra or being a soloist.

Like many musicians of his time, he also carried on some business activity to supplement his income. He acted as agent for Count Vincent Waldstein's export of timber and other goods.[3]

The Abel and Bach circle

Kammel belonged to the circle of musicians around Karl Friedrich Abel and Johann Christian Bach.

Karl Friedrich Abel came to London in 1763 and in 1775 obtained denization, thus becoming a British subject. His mother and her sister joined him in London where they both died in 1766.[4] He lodged with Bach in Meard Street until 1771, later on with a Mr. Herve, watch maker, in Greek Street, and finally with William Cramer, first in Carlisle Street, then at 201 Oxford Street and 6 Duke Street. He was very close to Bach. After Bach's death in 1782 he went to Germany, but returned in 1785 and carried on with his playing at concerts. He died in 1787.

Mrs. Papendiek, Assistant-Keeper of the Wardrobe and Reader to Her Majesty Queen Charlotte, said about him in her memoirs: "Abel pursued his professional studies and performances till within a few weeks of his death." The death of Bach affected Abel deeply. She went on to say: "Abel was eminent both as a composer and a player, but the season he

---

[1] Freemanová, Michaela & Mikanová, Eva (2003b) p.212
[2] Mozart, Wolfgang Amadeus (1776) v.1, ip.195, No.99. "Mr Kammel Violinist"
[3] Freemanova, Michaela (2001); Freemanová, Michaela & Mikanová, Eva (2003b)
[4] *Gentlemen's Magazine* Deaths 14 March 1766

Shugborough

• Cottesmore

• Stamford

• LONDON

• Bath   • Newbury   Faversham
             • Stratfield Saye   Norton • •   • Canterbury
                                  • Knole
Salisbury •   • Winchester

•
Blandford

Some locations associated with Kammel which
might not be found on all maps

lost his friend he lost also much of his power of exertion from grief, and often had recourse to stimulant that overdid his intention. One evening, at the Queen's concert, he was led to his seat, but he performed so admirably that the state he was in was not discovered by royalty".[5]

Johann Christian Bach also came to London in 1763. He lived in Meard Street, Queen Street and Carlisle Street. He married the famous singer Galli who, according to Mrs. Papendiek, "assisted him with her savings of £2,000".[6] He died in 1782.

Henry Angelo, the son of his neighbour, describes in his reminiscences

[5] Papendiek, Charlotte Louisa Henrietta (1887). v.1 pp.153-4
[6] Papendiek, Charlotte Louisa Henrietta (1887). v.1 p.109

how Bach and Abel used to visit his father: "Well do I remember the delightful evenings which for years were frequent under my paternal roof".[7]

Bach and Abel organized for a long time concerts in London which were later superseded by the professional concerts led by Cramer. Mrs. Papendiek describes Bach's reaction: "It was too evident that the decline of Bach's pre-eminence preyed upon his health, and his finances were in a worse state than he was at first aware of, which did not tend to ameliorate his distress".[8]

Later on she says: "Dear, amiable Bach, after being for several months in declining state, was now removed to Paddington for change of air".[9] He had few visitors. The Zoffanys and Abel supplied him with provisions and when he died "Mr. Papendiek, with the assistance of Bach's faithful coachman, kept creditors from disturbing the corpse". Bach's friends deserted him: "...no one among his musical associates came forward with any offer of respect, either public or private, and this great patron was carried to the grave and buried with the attendance only of four friends, my father, Mr. Papendiek, Zoffany, and Bautebart, but they were indeed sincere mourners".[10]

The main patron of Bach and Abel's concerts was **Willoughby Bertie, 4th Earl of Abingdon.** He provided a substantial proportion of the funding for the concerts. There is no evidence that he would have had any personal contact with Kammel.

Concerts in 18th century London

Concert life in eighteenth century London is well documented.

Kammel belonged to a world which "included the landed nobility and gentry ('the quality'), but it also incorporated a range of professionals, clergy and men of letters; indeed anyone who could pass himself off as a well educated gentleman".[11] By his residence, social standing and performances he belonged to the "Westminster" half of London.

[7] Angelo, Henry. *Reminiscences*, London: Colburn, 1830 2v p.19
[8] Papendiek, Charlotte Louisa Henrietta (1887) v.1 p.133
[9] Papendiek, Charlotte Louisa Henrietta (1887) v.1 p.150
[10] Papendiek, Charlotte Louisa Henrietta (1887) v.1 p.151
[11] McVeigh, Simon. (1993) *Concert life in London from Mozart to Haydn*, Cambridge: Cambridge University Press 1993, p.11

He was closely associated with the Bach-Abel subscription concerts. He also participated in benefit concerts. Unfortunately, there is no information as to the programmes of the Bach-Abel concerts and therefore we cannot tell which ones Kammel performed at.[12] However, considering his closeness to Bach and Abel it is likely that he played regularly with them. Curiously enough, Johann Christian Bach's financial documents at the Drummond Bank do not list Kammel as a recipient of money. He may have been paid in cash or he was playing for free to return a service.

Although an early 19th century report rates the concerts highly, their existence was precarious: "In 1764, Bach and Abel's concerts were established where the best pieces and composers were heard...These entertainments were very prosperous till 1780, when they began to decline; and Lord Abingdon, for several seasons, gave the conductors pecuniary assistance, to secure them from loss, to the amount of £1,600".[13]

Concerts were also organized by various musical societies in the City, but musicians shunned them when something better turned up.[14] The City concerts were designed for the "wealthier bourgeois of the City"[15] and were not advertised. Judging by his lifestyle, Kammel liked to be considered part of "Westminster" society. However, he did have things in common with the people of the "City", since he was supplementing his income as a commercial contact for his patron Count Vincent Waldstein. He had an account at the Bank of England and in his Will he wished his sons to be apprenticed for a trade.

Some aspects of the running of concerts emerge in the advertisements, stating whether tickets had to be purchased in advance or could be bought at the door: "No person will be admitted without ticket, and no tickets but those of the night will positively be admitted".[16] Some advertisements give an explanation of postponement due, for instance, to an inability to get a suitable room in time.

It seems that London's evening life was not free from traffic congestion and that there was a need for regulating coaches: "The nobility and gentry are advised to order their coachmen to set them down at the

[12] McVeigh, Simon. (1993) p.119
[13] Stafford, William. *A history of music.* Edinburgh: Constable, 1830, pp.268-9
[14] McVeigh, Simon. (1993) p.38
[15] McVeigh, Simon. (1993) p.3, pp.32-35
[16] *Public Advertiser* 18 April 1769

usual door, with the horses heads towards St James's Street; and to take them up in the like manner at the new door near the square, as the other door will be only for the Chairs![17]

Some concerts were held in private houses. Elizabeth Harris wrote in a letter:

"Yesterday morning we were all at that most elegant house at Mr Ansons to a breakfast and concert after, every thing suited the elegance of the house. When breakfast was ended the rooms were all open for people to walk about and admire – after that the concert, for which he had collected the best hands in Town".[18]

It is possible that, between 1773 and 1775 Anthony Kammel himself organized some Friday subscription concerts. Evidence can be found in the London accounts of James Harris.[19]

The sale of tickets was done through the performers and various agents listed in the advertisements. The number of ticket selling points in each advertisement suggested the degree of intensity of promotion. Most advertisements had one or two, while only three had as many as five. In about a quarter of Kammel's concerts it was Kammel himself, in another quarter Welcker's Music Shop, in another various music shops, taverns and coffee places and in the remainder performers other than Kammel.

The main music shops in the Kammel concerts period (1768-1782) were Bremner's in the Strand, Johnson's in Cheapside, Napier's in the Strand, Smith's in Piccadilly, Thorogood's in the Royal Exchange, and Welcker's in Gerrard Street, later in Haymarket.

Eating and entertainment places associated with the selling of tickets for Kammel's concerts were: Jack's Coffee House in Dean Street, Marchi's Italian Warehouse in the Haymarket, The Orange Coffee House in the Haymarket, The St. Alban's Tavern near Pall Mall, The Sun Tavern in Berkeley Square, and The Thatched House Tavern in St James's Street.

---

[17] *Public Advertiser* 18 April 1769
[18] Burrows, Donald & Dunhill, Rosemary (2001) 24 March 1772
[19] Burrows, Donald & Dunhill, Rosemary (2001) p.760 note; Burrows, Donald & Dunhill, Rosemary (2001) p.832; Burrows, Donald & Dunhill, Rosemary (2001) p.1012

Kammel's concerts in London

Between 1768 and 1782 Anthony Kammel took part in 31 concerts in London. A complete list is given in Appendix I. The information comes from the *Calendar of London Concerts 1750-1800 advertised in the London Daily Press*[20], and is supplemented from the notes collected by Zdeňka Pilková, and from other published sources.

Nine of them were benefit concerts in his name, six in his name jointly with somebody else. The flutist Karl Weiss shared three benefit concerts with him.

It was a custom among some musicians to play at each other's benefit concerts and the same group of musicians met year after year.

The musicians with whom Kammel performed most frequently - Fischer (19), Bach (16), Crosdill (14), Abel (13), Cramer (9), Weiss (6), Tenducci (5) - were his closest collaborators and, presumably, his friends.

During the last three years of this period, the number of Kammel's concerts had gone down due, quite likely to his age and ill health.

The total number of concerts listed in Appendix I seems rather low, because the list is limited to his musical activity recorded in documents - in the newspapers or in contemporary reminiscences. Other concerts were not recorded in print.

Kammel's concerts out of London

In 1768 and 1769 Kammel gave three concerts in **Bath**,[21] in 1773 and 1774 two concerts at **Blandford**.[22]

In 1775 Kammel dedicated his Six Dancing Minuets (without Opus number) to "a select assembly at Newberry". In the absence of written records it is fair to assume the concerts took place at the **Newberry Mansion House**[23] which the Duchess of Devonshire used to visit with her

---

[20] printout kindly supplied by Simon McVeigh
[21] Freemanová, Michaela & Mikanová, Eva (2003b); Burchell (1996) pp.123-4
[22] Freemanová, Michaela & Mikanová, Eva (2003b) p.229
[23] Paul Cannon, the Visitor Services Officer at heritage@westberks.gov.uk has supplied the following information: The Mansion House in Newbury was completed in 1740 or 1742 and demolished in 1908. As you will see it contained the room in which assemblies were held:

relative, Stephen Poyntz, who used to live at Midgham House. A nineteenth century historian says that "the family party from Midgham House used to be frequent attenders at the monthly ball, held at the Mansion House of Newbury".[24]

Another historian confirms it: "When Mr. Poyntz resided at Midgham the famous Duchess of Devonshire, the Countess of Bessborough, the Margravine of Anspach, and other ladies of distinction, made it a point of attending the Newbury balls, and of mixing with those of humbler birth, in order to give éclat to these assemblages, and to promote a good feeling between all classes. The subscription for the season was ten shillings; and the balls began at seven and ended at twelve o'clock precisely - a regulation which was rigorously enforced".[25]

In 1770 Kammel dedicated his Op.4 to George Pitt who lived at **Stratfield Saye House**, about 15 miles from Newbury. Kammel's eldest child Lucy was born there on 11 December 1769. As all his other children were born in London, it was probably the only occasion when his pregnant wife accompanied him during his travels. Travel by coach was uncomfortable and at times dangerous. Mrs. Papendiek describes how her coach was robbed on the way between Kew and St. James's: "I saw three men run up from the waterside. One went to the horses' heads, while one came to each side of the carriage, opened the doors, and demanded our money".[26] Ann Kammel must have been very brave indeed to travel with her husband in an advanced stage of her first pregnancy.

Kammel used to visit **Salisbury** regularly during the annual Music Festival there, giving concerts in 1771, 1772, 1774, 1775, 1776 and 1782.[27]

"Erected in 1742, it is supported on piers and arches, the lower part affords an area for the butter and poultry market, and the upper part consists of a handsome suite of rooms, in the largest of which the courts are held and assemblies during the season; it is a spacious and very handsome room, adorned with paintings; adjoining it are refreshment and card rooms".
[24] Goodwin, Henry. *The Worthies and celebrities connected with Newbury, Berkshire and its neighbourhood*, Newbury: J. Blacket, 1859 p.49
[25] Money, Walter. *The History of the ancient town and borough of Newbury, in the county of Berkshire*, Oxford: Parker & Co., 1887, p.379; he also refers to new chandeliers for 1770
[26] Papendiek, Charlotte Louisa Henrietta (1887) p.123
[27] Freemanová, Michaela & Mikanová, Eva (2003b); Burrows (2001) p.893, p.851; review in Salisbury Journal 9 October 1775

In the papers of the Harris family we read:

"Our great Music Festival was last week. Our rehearsals were as usual excellent, music and company more than the rooms could contain: the overflowing stood in the long passage and had the liberty of speech".[28]

The impressive spire of Salisbury Cathedral as Kammel would have known it

On two occasions, in 1770 and 1778, Kammel gave a concert at the **Winchester** Music Festival.[29]

---

[28] Burrows, Donald & Dunhill, Rosemary (2001) p.851
[29] Freemanová, Michaela & Mikanová, Eva (2003b) p.220

It is surprising that there are no records of any of his concerts in **Kent,** although he had visited the county more than once and there was a music society in Canterbury. Three of Kammel's friends lived in Kent: John Cockin (or Cockain or Cockayne) Sole who was a Sheriff of Kent and lived at the seat of his wife's family, Norton Court. Two of his neighbours were Joseph Banks at a house called Provender near to the present day Norton Ash, and Horatio Mann at Bourne, about twenty miles east of Norton.

In one of his letters to Count Vincent Waldstein Kammel wrote about his period of convalescence at Horatio Mann's house.[30] He described the company there: "...The whole Mann family was publicly toasting the health of Your Excellency. The whole family, Esq. Tay[lor], Mr Sole and George Pitt are, unknown to you, sending their best regards".[31]

In November 1765, before being taken by him to visit Horatio Mann, Kammel was staying in the house of his new patron, Mr Tay[lor]. The name transcribed from the quoted letter, which I have not seen, is probably illegible. It is likely that it was Henry Roper Baron of Teynham (also spelled Tenham) whose seat Lynsted was very near to Norton Court. Norton Court, Provender House and the villages of Lynsted and Tenham form a cluster of places about a mile apart from each other. Bourne is about 20 miles east of them.[32]

There was another person to whom Kammel dedicated his composition in 1780 and who lived nearby. It was the Duke of Dorset who had his house at Knole about 20 miles from Sittingbourne in Kent. He was a friend of Horatio Mann and shared his interest in cricket.

---

[30] Freemanová, Michaela & Mikanová, Eva (2003b) p.216
[31] Freemanová, Michaela (2001) p.18
[32] Freemanová, Michaela & Mikanová, Eva (2003b) p.215

Provender House, Norton, as it stands today

Reviews of Kammel's music making

Before coming to Britain, during his concerts in Prague, Kammel was much praised for his "cantilena" playing.[33]

He was subsequently very popular during his visits to Salisbury. The audience liked him. Elizabeth Harris, wrote in her letter:

"Your father and Louisa went to Kammells benefit at the Festino rooms, and they were in as great a crowd; almost all Salisbury are in Town".[34]

The advertisements for his Salisbury concerts were full of superlatives:

"Mr. Kammell, so celebrated for his musical skill, will lead the band as first violin".[35]

and he had mostly good reviews.

---

[33] Dlabač, Jan Bohumír (1815) v.2. p.38; Lhota, A. *Rakovnicko českému životu hudebnímu, Rakovnické noviny*, 1940 p.11; Gerber, Ernst Ludwig (1790) v.3 p.20
[34] Burrows, Donald & Dunhill, Rosemary (2001) p.893
[35] *Salisbury Journal* 14 September 1772

A review of his 1775 concert says:

"...the instrumental by Mr. Fischer, Mr. Kammell, Mr. Cervetto, Mr. Tewksbury and Mr. Gehot; who all performed their several parts with such accuracy, taste, and judgment, as gaining the highest applause from as numerous and polite an audience as ever was known upon the like occasion ... The audience at the Rooms in the three nights were near one thousand in number, and in the two days at the cathedral upwards of five hundred".[36]

However, in 1776 John Marsh recorded in his diary his disappointment with Kammel's playing:

"...in the evening we went to the 1st performance at the Rooms being Grand Miscellaneous Concert, led by Kammell; in whom (having heard much of him as a composer of duetts, trios, etc) I was rather disappointed, as he by no means as professor seem'd to rank above mediocrity; our own leader Tewksbury as well as many gent'n performers being equal and some superior to him. By way of a solo, he played a piece so very tame and little interesting, and displaying so small a degree of execution, that Dr. Stevens was I remember much disconcerted at it and said it was an insult to the audience".[37]

It is possible that Kammel's performance had been affected by his ill health. Some of his letters to Count Vincent Waldstein indicate that he suffered, among other things, from arthritis and depression. The precise nature of his illness and the cause of his death is not known.[38]

The most negative review, dated 1780, was from the pen of an anonymous author who called himself ABC Dario: "K – a German, formerly (he says) an officer in the Prussian service. He has published several works, which Mr. Bach has, with great good-nature, assisted him in, as he has done for others. As a performer on the violin, his talents are below mediocrity; and though he has composed for the harpsichord, we know his talent for that instrument is on a par with his violin performance".[39]

---

[36] *Salisbury Journal* 9 October 1775
[37] Marsh, John (1998) p.147]
[38] Mikanová, Eva (1989) p.143; Freemanová, Michaela (2001) p.18
[39] *ABC Dario* (1780) p.31

Kammel had been considered a celebrity in Shougborough, the home of Thomas Anson.

On April 25th 1772 Sir William Bagot wrote a poem to welcome Thomas Anson back from London. He included Kammel's name in the poem:

"Bring Attic Stuart, Indian Orme,
Kammell unruffled by a storm
Shall tune his softest strain;
And my Louisa will rejoice
To notes like his to tune her voice
With health restored again".[40]

Simon McVeigh thinks that "The Bohemian violinist, pupil of Tartini, was a popular composer but he never achieved eminence as a performer ... It should be pointed out, however, that even when such as Cramer, Giardini or Stamitz took part in his benefit Kammell still played a solo or concerto on the violin, or else (from 1774) a viola solo ... This suggests a considerably higher standard of attainment".[41]

As to Kammel's compositions, Zdeňka Pilková, writing about Kammel's achievement, says: "Kammel belonged, in his time, to those composers whose works were played and published very often. Most of his compositions appeared in print: between the years 1770 and 1783 they were reprinted many times by leading publishers in London, Paris, Amsterdam, The Hague and Berlin. After 1786 his works appeared in print very rarely, he was almost completely forgotten. Nor has music historiography in recent decades, which in an attempt to explain in greater detail the genesis of the classical style has rediscovered many forgotten personalities of this period, devoted much attention to Anthony Kammel".[42]

And what did Kammel think of himself? He included descriptions of his concerts in his regular letters to Count Vincent Waldstein, giving an impression that modesty was not one of his virtues.

On March 11, 1766 Kammel wrote:

"Several weeks ago I played in my first public concert with such

---

[40] www.shugborough.org.uk/AcademyGreekRevival2-178
[41] McVeigh, Simon (1989) p.85
[42] Pilkova, Zdeňka. Manuscript in private archive

30

applause which I had not expected, Giardini and others were beaten, my work goes well ... if I would be allowed to stay here one year more, I could have a benefit concert in the next year, which would certainly bring me 100 pounds Stirling...".[43]

And in January 1767:

"In a public concert I played 2 solos and the clapping was such as I never had in my life; [there was] Mann himself, young and old ladies and Misses ... all of them in love, and I made them even more loving through my old violin, and [I myself] was the second day very much in love with one young lady...".[44]

In some of his later letters there are indications of his health problems. In June 18th 1774 he wrote:

"...My benefit concert was also not the best one, as I hardly was able to walk, and was not able to play myself, I had to leave somebody else to lead, and almost all I gained was devoured by 3 pigtailed doctor's wigs".[45]

Miss Edicatt's concerts

Miss Lydia Edicatt was one of the younger sisters of Kammel's wife Ann.

She sang at three Kammel benefit concerts: in 1778, 1779 and 1780.

During the five years between 1778 and 1783 she performed at 6 London concerts, mostly at the Tottenham Street Rooms. Her last concert took place at the Freemasons Hall on 10th March 1783. The review of her last concert, conducted by Solomon, was negative: "This lady seemed to be indisposed, and could not give a full scope to her vocal powers".[46]

Less than two weeks later, Lydia Edicatt married a German merchant Charles Christian Besser and left the musical scene.

---

[43] Freemanová, Michaela & Mikanová, Eva (2003b) p.216
[44] Freemanová, Michaela & Mikanová, Eva (2003b) p.216
[45] Freemanová, Michaela & Mikanová, Eva (2003b) p.222
[46] *Morning Post* 11 March 1783

Court music

Various sources mention that Kammel was a member of the Court orchestra. There are no records confirming it. However, he might have deputised for some of the violinists in the King's Band or obtained other engagements through them.

Members of the Royal family had a strong interest in music. Mrs. Papendiek, Assistant-Keeper of the Wardrobe and Reader to Her Majesty Queen Charlotte, describes musical parties held on Tuesdays and Thursdays from eight till ten o'clock to which between two and three hundred people were invited. There was also a lot of chamber music played, with members of the Royal family, particularly the Prince of Wales, taking part. A quartet party used to meet once a fortnight.

There is no record of any connection between court musicians and Kammel, except for the following:

William Boyce was associated with the Salisbury Festival and could have arranged for Kammel to lead the orchestra.

John Crosdill appeared in 13 London concerts with Kammel. Miss Edicott [sic] sang at his benefit concerts in 1778 and 1779.[47]

Crosdill lived in Titchfield Street. In 1769 tickets for Kammel's concerts were sold at a corner of Gt. Titchfield Street, which could have been John Crosdill's residence. He later moved to Grosvenor Square. In 1785 he married a rich wife, Elizabeth Colebrooke, and retired from music. Various reference books have mistaken Kammel for Crosdill, stating that Kammel had married a rich wife.

Francis Hackwood lived in 10 Half Moon Street between 1768 and 1781. A year later he joined the King's Band and moved to no.35 Half Moon Street, next door to Anthony Kammel.[48]

Robert Rawlings (Rawlins) travelled Europe for 9 years with the Duke of York as his musical page until 1767. He could have met Anthony Kammel on his travels. On his return to England he became a violinist in the King's and Queen's bands. He was possibly the musician for whom Kammel substituted.

---

[47] *Public Advertiser* May 1778, May 1779
[48] Parke, William Thomas. *Musical memoirs*, 2v, London, 1830, v.1, p.103

Kammel's pupils

Only two names of Kammel's pupils are mentioned in printed sources: Benjamin Blake and Joseph Obermayer.

Benjamin Blake studied with Kammel and Cramer and became a member of the King's Theatre Orchestra.

Joseph Obermayer is said to have studied with Kammel in Bohemia.

It seems unlikely, however, that Kammel had only two pupils. In a letter to Count Vincent Waldstein dated 2 March 1773 Kammel wrote:

"I work from early morning to the night – sometimes up to 12 p.m. or even 1 a.m. In the morning I have [my] pupils from whom I have half-a-Guinea for one lesson...".[49]

Other musician friends of Kammel

William Cramer gave 8 London concerts with Kammel.
John Christian Fischer gave 17 concerts with Kammel.
Giusto Ferdinando Tenducci gave 5 London concerts with Kammel.
Karl Weiss gave 6 London concerts with Kammel.

Kammel's membership of societies

Anthony Kammel, like many other musicians of the time, was a **Freemason**.

The Somerset House Lodge had a strong musical tradition. Bach, Abel and Cramer joined the Lodge of the Nine Muses in 1777.

Kammel himself in 1779 became a member of the newly founded Pilgrim Lodge - the only German-speaking lodge in London started by the German businessman Johan Leonhardi [1747-1830].[50]

He was not a member of **The Royal Society of Musicians**, nor of **The Worshipful Company of Musicians**.

---

[49] Freemanová, Michaela & Mikanová, Eva (2003b) p.221
[50] McVeigh, Simon (2000)

Kammel's published works in Britain

This chapter draws on the holdings of Kammel's printed music in the British Library, the British Union Catalogue of Early Music, the Longman & Broderip catalogues of music for sale in the late eighteenth century, the sales catalogue of the Moffat Music Library, the 1784 Musikalischer Almanach published in Germany and the collections of French and Dutch music catalogues edited by Johansson.[1]

Kammel's works were published between 1764 and 1784. The dates of some of the publications are estimates as they were not given on the title page. The places of publication were London, Paris, Amsterdam, The Hague and Berlin. Some works appeared in several editions or variants by different publishers, and some contained discrepancies in numbering, particularly of opus numbers.

Some London publications had French title pages, which is puzzling and suggests we may be dealing with variants – intended either for export or for sale to the French expatriate community.

Apart from the published compositions, manuscript copies of Kammel's works can be found in various archives, particularly in the libraries of Czech monasteries and castles. Some of these were copied from published material, others not. Kammel's unpublished manuscripts are, however, outside the scope of this chapter.

Occasionally, Kammel edited works for other composers (e.g. in London in 1773 he published six overtures by various authors, among them Jan Václav Stamic and Johan Baptist Vaňhal).

---

[1] http://catalogue.bl.uk; *The British Union Catalogue of Early Music Printed before 1801*, ed. B. Schnapper, 2 vols. Butterworth Scientific Publications, 1957; *A Complete Catalogue of Instrumental and Vocal Music Printed and Sold by Longman and Broderip*, 1789, BL 1601/587; *The Valuable Music Library Formed by Alfred Moffat, Esq.* BL Hirsch 466; *Musikalischer Almanach fur Deutschland auf das Jahr 1784*, BL Hirsch IV.1123; Johansson C. *French Music Publishers' Catalogues*, 1955 BL Ac.5150.b.

Kammel's published compositions

Op.1. *Sei Trii di Violino e Basso / Six Sonates à Deux Violons et Basse*

The British Library has three versions of this composition dedicated to "Lady Lucy Mann".

The preface to the earliest edition of *Sei Trii di Violino e Basso*[2] is dated 15 March 1766. It was most likely a self-publication by the composer. It is listed in the sales catalogue of the Moffat Music Library as having no publisher. Apart from the British Library it is at the King's College Library, Cambridge.

A reissue under the same Italian title by P. Welcker in London was published in 1770. The British Library has two copies.[3] The title plate of the first edition was reused and the opus number "Opera Prima" replaced with publication details. There is an advertisement for Op.2, published by P. Welcker circa 1770, which suggests a publication in the early part of the year or earlier. Apart from the British Library it is at the London University Library, King's College Library, Cambridge, Pendlebury Library, Cambridge, Royal Academy of Music, and Bodleian Library, Oxford. The copy in the Library of Congress is probably this edition.

The composition was later published, again under the same Italian title, by S. A. & P. Thompson in London in 1780[4], re-using the plate of the previous edition and substituting the name of the new publisher. It was sold at Fortnum's Music Shop. Apart from the British Library it is at the King's College Library, Cambridge and at the Manchester Public Library.

There was a Dutch publication by Hummel entitled *Trio à Deux Violons, Flute trav. & Basse* advertised in the B. Hummel 1768 catalogue. As there is no copy in British libraries, it has not been possible to ascertain whether the Dutch publication came out in 1768 in parallel with the first London publication, or if it was earlier. A 1775 B. Hummel publication of the work is at the British Library with the title *Six Sonates à Deux Violons et Basse*.[5]

---

[2] BL g .242.(12)
[3] BL g.415.(4); R.M.17.c.6.(9.)
[4] BL g .420.e.(3)
[5] BL h .1909.a

Op.2. *Six Duets for Two Violins / Six Sonates à Deux Violons / Six Duettos à Deux Violons/ Six Duets pour Deux Violins / Six Sonates a Deux Violons*

The British Library has four versions of this composition.

The first British edition, *Six Duets for Two Violins,* was published by P. Welcker in London cca.1770.[6] Apart from the British Library it is at the Royal Academy of Music in London.

The Moffat Music Library sales catalogue gives an earlier edition by B. Hummel in The Hague and Amsterdam in 1767. The B. Hummel catalogues of 1769 and 1771 list the composition as one of their own publications, dated 1768. The 1772 De La Chevardière catalogue in Paris lists it as its own undated publication; *Six Duets pour Deux Violins;* of which the British Library has a copy.[7] A later 1775 issue by Hummel with a French title *Six Sonates à Deux Violons* is also at the British library.[8] The British Library has another Amsterdam edition called *Six Duettos à Deux Violons* by S. Markoldt Amsterdam dated cca.1770.[9] The Musikalischer Almanach 1784 gives the place of publication as Amsterdam. According to the British Union Catalogue of Early Music, the Royal College of Music has an edition called *Six Sonates à Deux Violons* published by M. Götz in Mannheim.

A later British edition in the British Library with the title *Six Duets for Two Violins* was published in 1778 by S. A. & P. Thompson in London.[10] The Longman and Broderip London catalogues of 1778, 1781 and 1789 list a *Duet for Two Violins* as their own publication calling it Op.no.11. As the first edition had the opus number in Roman numerals, the no.11 could be a printing error.

Op.3. *A Second Sett of Six Sonatas for Two Violins and a Bass*

The British Library has two versions of this composition dedicated to "Count Vincent of Waldstein".

The first British edition was published by P. Welcker in 1769 in London under the title *A Second Sett of Six Sonatas for Two Violins and a*

---

[6] BL g .421.d.(1)
[7] BL g.218.ff.(3.)
[8] BL g .411.(3)
[9] BL g .218.u.(1)
[10] BL g .218.z.(4)

36

Bass.[11] There is some doubt as to the dating of this publication: If Op.2 advertised on the title page is dated 1770, then it is unlikely that Op.3 would be dated 1769. The date given in the New Grove is 1770. Apart from the British Library it is at the King's College Library, Cambridge, Pendlebury Library, Cambridge, London University Library, and Bodleian Library, Oxford.

There is a 1780 edition with the same title by the London firm of Longman and Broderip.[12] It could have been a reprint of the earlier P. Welcker publication with a new publisher on the title page. It is listed in the Longman and Broderip London catalogues of 1781 and 1789, either under its full name or under "Trios". A composition under the name of "Trios" is also offered in a Longman and Broderip 1778 catalogue. This could be the first edition under an abridged title.

The catalogues of the various Continental music publishers list three works which, under different titles, probably contain versions of this composition: B. Hummel's Hague catalogue of 1770 lists *Six sonates, 2vl & b* Op.3, his 1771 catalogue lists *Trios a 2 Violons & Basse*, Op.3, Venier's Paris catalogue of 1773 *Duetti per Due Violini*, and Le Menu et Boyer's Paris catalogue of 1772 *Trio Op.3*.

Op.4. Six Quartettos for Two Violins à Tenor and Violoncello Obligato / Six Quatuors à Deux Violons, Alto et Violoncello Obligés / Six Quautors [sic] Concertante à Deux Violons, Alto et Violoncelle / Six Quatuors a 2 Violons, Taille et Basse Obligés

The British Library has two versions of this composition dedicated to "His Excellency George Pitt, Esq.", the first one in two copies.

The first British edition of this work, *Six Quartettos for Two Violins a Tenor and Violoncello Obligato* was published by P. Welcker in London in 1770.[13] Apart from the British Library it is at the King's College Library, Cambridge, the Royal Academy of Music, London University Library, Manchester Public Library and the Bodleian Library, Oxford. A copy of this edition is probably in the Library of Congress.

---

[11] BL g .222.h.(1)
[12] BL g .420.e.(5)
[13] BL g.411.(1); R.M.16.f.14.(13)

Six

QUARTETTOS

for two

VIOLINS a TENOR and

VIOLONCELLO OBLIGATO

moſt humbly Dedicated

To His Excellency

GEORGE PITT ESQ.ᴿ

His Majesty's Ambaſsador Extraordinary and Minister Plenipotentiary to the Court of **Spain**

Compoſed by

ANTONIO KAMMELL

OPERA IV.

LONDON Printed by WELCKER in Gerrard Street S.ᵗ Ann's Soho
Where may be had by the ſame Author two Setts of Trios and a Sett of Duetts.
Juſt Publiſhed a ſecond Sett of Six Harpſichord Concertos by Bach Six Overtures being the
ſecond Sett by Pugnani. N.B. Garths Jeſſons & Marcellos Pſalms with the greateſt Choice of Muſic.

Cover page from Opus 4 work as published by Welcker of London

A later edition was published by Wornum in London in 1775 with a French title page *Six Quatuors à Deux Violons, Alto et Violoncello obligés.*[14] It is very likely a reissue of the Welcker edition after P. Welcker's death. Longman and Broderip London offered it for sale as their own publication in their catalogues of 1778, 1781 and 1789 under the name of *Quartets*.

---

[14] BL h .1909.b

On the Continent, B. Hummel in The Hague offered for sale a publication called *Ouverture* Op.4 in his 1771 catalogue. The 1770 catalogue of Huberty in Paris calls it *Six Quautors [sic] Concertante à Deux Violons, Alto et Violoncelle* and the 1779 catalogue of De La Cheverdière in Paris lists it as *Quatuors* Op.4. The Musikalischer Almanach gives Amsterdam as the place of publication of the *Six Quatuors a 2 Violons, Taille et Basse Obligées*, Op.4.

[No Op.] *Six Trio Sonatas Arranged for Harpsichord, Violin and Violoncello by Charles Roeser*

The British Library does not have this composition.

In the early 1770s Charles Roeser arranged Kammel's sonatas. The New Grove lists a 1770 publication of *Six sonatas, 2vn b* arr. C. Roeser. Another 1780 publication entitled *Six sonates, hpd, vn, b* could be a later edition of the same work. Both were published in Paris. The Le Menu et Boyer Paris catalogue of 1775 offered the publication for sale as *Pièces de Clavecin*.

Op.5. *Six Duetts for Two Violins / Sechs Violinduetten*

The British Library has two versions of this composition dedicated to "Thomas Anson, Esq."

It was published cca.1770 under the title *Six Duetts for Two Violins* by P. Welcker in London.[15] However, according to the sale catalogue of the Moffat Music Library, it was first published by the composer himself in 1768. The New Grove dictionary also gives the publication date as 1768. A copy of the 1768 edition is in the British Library with manuscript notes by Andrew Moffat on the endpapers: "The imprint on the present edition shows it to be the first edition".[16] However, there is a query about the composer's address. It is given on the title page as Half-Moon Street – the address where Kammel did not move to until 1770. Massinghi's Italian Warehouse was given as the retail outlet.

Of the Continental versions, there is only one publication in the Sieber Paris catalogue of 1772 called *Duo* Op.5. In 1784 the Musikalischer

---

[15] BL g .421.d.(2)
[16] BL g .276.d

Almanach listed a publication called *Sechs Violinduetten*, Op.5.

[No Op] Six overtures in Eight Parts by the following composers, I. Stamitz, II. Vanhall, III. Mislevecheck, IV. Princess Royal of Saxony, V. Hayden, VI. Vanhall, the whole collected by Antonio Kammel (arrangement)

The British Library has one copy of this collection.

In the early 1770s Kammel arranged and edited six overtures by contemporary composers, published in London by P. Welcker in 1773. [17] Apart from the British Library, the publication is at the Royal College of Music, London.

A later edition was published in London by S. A. & P. Thompson in 1790. It is in the King's College Library, Cambridge.

Op.6. *Six Notturnos for Two Violins and a Bass / Six Notturnos à Deux Violons et Basse / Trio per Due Violini & Basso*

The British Library has three versions of this composition dedicated to "Lady Young of Delaford".

The work, *Six Notturnos for Two Violins and a Bass*, was first published by the composer and by P. Welcker in 1772 in London.[18] The version published by Welcker is at the King's College Library, Cambridge, Pendelbury Library, Cambridge, and the Bodleian Library Oxford. The version published by the author is at the British Library, the King's College Library Cambridge, and the Bodleian Library, Oxford.

It was reissued under the same title by P. Welcker in 1775 in London[19] and by Longman and Broderip in 1780 in London.[20] The 1775 publication is listed in the Longman & Broderip, London 1778 catalogue as their own publication, the 1780 one in their 1781 and 1789 catalogues. The later version is also at King's College Library, Cambridge. The Welcker edition uses the original title page with a

---

[17] BL g .474.(7)
[18] BL h .2782.gg.(3)
[19] BL h .2900.(3)
[20] BL g .420.e.(4)

change as to price and publisher. The Longman and Broderip copy carries a Fentnum sticker.

Cover page from the Venier, Paris, publication of Opus 6

The British Union List of Early Music records also a 1790 edition by J. Preston in London. A copy of it is at the Oxford University Faculty Library.

The Moffat Music Library sale catalogue suggests that the first London publication was preceded in 1770 by that of S. Markoldt in Amsterdam under the title *Six Notturnos à Deux Violons et Basse* Op.6. A copy of it can be found in the King's College Library, Cambridge. Venier Paris listed a copy of *Trio* Op.6 in his catalogue of 1771 and *Trio per Due Violini & Basso li qualli si potranno esequire e piena orchestra*, Op.6 in his catalogue of 1773. The B. Hummel's catalogues list *Six Sonatines 2vl & b* Op.6 in 1772 and *Trios à 2 Violons et Basse* Op.6 in 1773.

[No Op.] *A Third Sett of Trios or Ballo, Consisting of Two Acts*

The British Library has one copy of this composition.

In the mid-1770s *A Third sett of Trios or Ballo, consisting of two Acts with a short introductory Overture to each Act and a Collection of Airs* without an opus number was published by P. Welcker in London.[21] The date was approximately 1774, although the New Grove gives it as approximately 1770. Judging by the compositions advertised on the title page, the more likely date is 1774.

Op.7. *A Second Sett of Six Quartettos for Two Violins a Tenor and Violoncello Obligato / Six Quatuors à Deux Violons Taille et Basse/ Six Sonates à Deux Violons et Basse / Sechs Sonaten für 2 Violinen*

The British Library has one copy of this composition dedicated to "The Right Honourable the Countess Spencer".

This composition, *A Second Sett of Six Quartettos for Two Violins à Tenor and Violoncello Obligato*, was first published in London by P. Welcker in 1775.[22] Apart from the British Library it is at the Cambridge University Library, the King's College Library Cambridge and the Manchester Public Library. The copy in the Library of Congress is probably this edition.

In a Longman & Broderip London catalogue of 1778 it is advertised as *Trio* Op.7 although it is a quartet. The New Grove gives three compositions as Op.7: *Six Quartetos, 2vn, va, vc*, Op.7 published in London, *Concert du violon,acc.2 vn, va, vc*, Op.7 published in Paris, and

---

[21] BL g.270.v.(2)
[22] BL g.276.a.(1)

Six Sonatas, 2vn, Op.7 published in The Hague. The Sieber Paris catalogue of 1772 lists a *Duo* as Op.7. This suggests some error in numbering: on the one hand Op.7 is described as a quartett, on the other as a duo and a trio.[23]

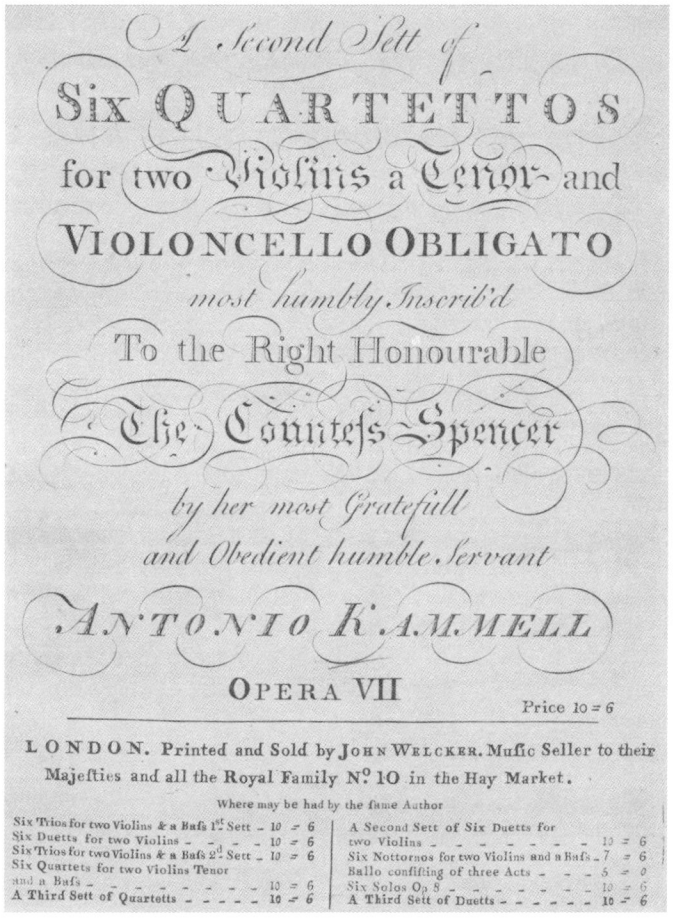

Another Welcker, London, publication, this of the Opus 7 along with dedication to "The Right Honourable The Countess Spencer"

---

[23] In the 18th century, trio sonatas were 3 instruments plus continuo/figured bass

According to the British Union Catalogue of Early Music there are two Dutch editions: *Six Sonates à Deux Violons et Basse* Op.7 published by B. Hummel in The Hague in 1775 and *Six Quatuors à Deux Violons, Taille et Basse* Op.7 published by J. Schmidt in Amsterdam in 1780. The latter is erroneously described as Op.8, possibly being due to a cataloguer's attempt to sort out the two works. The 1775 B. Hummel edition is at the King's College Library Cambridge and the British Library.[24] The J. Schmidt publication is in the British Library. The opus number on the title page is 8th, but a note in the British Library catalogue states it should be 7th.[25] The Musikalischer Almanach of 1784 gives it as *Sechs Sonaten für 2 Violinen*, Op.7 published in The Hague.

[No Op.] *Six Sonatas for Two Violins and a Violoncello, with a Thorough Bass for the Harpsichord ... composed by Messr Bach, Abel & Kammel*

The British Library has three copies of this composition.

In the mid-1770s a collection of trios by Bach, Abel and Kammel entitled Six sonatas for two violins and a violoncello, with a thorough bass for the harpsichord was published by J. Welcker in London.[26] The British Library catalogue gives the date as 1777, the British Union Catalogue of Early Music as 1775. Apart from the British Library it is at the King's College Library, Cambridge. The New Grove dates it as 1780.

The J. J. Hummel Hague 1778 catalogue offers it as its own publication under the title *Trios à 2 violons et basse - Bach, Abel, Kammel*, dated 1778.

Op.8. *Six Solos for the Violin with a Thorough Bass for the Harpsichord / Six Quatuor / Sechs Quarteten*

The British Library has one copy of this composition dedicated to "Richard Ottley Esq.".

Six Solos for the Violin with a Thorough Bass for the Harpsichord was

---

[24] BL g .276.c
[25] BL g .276.a.(2)
[26] BL g .415.(1); g.420.e.(6.); R.M.17,c,3.(14.)

published by P. Welcker in London in 1775.[27] Apart from the British Library it is at the King's College Library, Cambridge. Presumably the copy in the Library of Congress is of this edition.

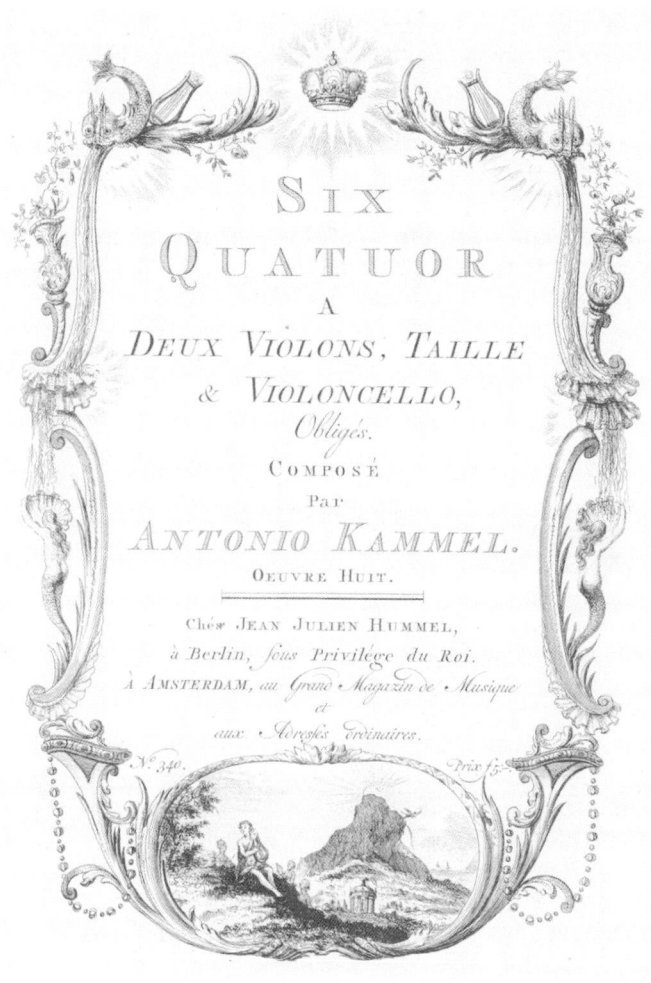

The rather ornate title page to the Hummel of Berlin, publication of the Opus 8 as listed in the 1774 catalogue

[27] BL h .1909

Longman listed it in the 1781 catalogue under the title *Violin Solos.*

There was a later edition in London by J. Preston in 1785. It is at the King's College Library, Cambridge.

There is some opus numbering confusion in the listings of three Continental publications. Sieber's Paris catalogue of 1772 lists *Trio* Op.8 and B. Hummel's Berlin catalogue of 1774 *Six Quatuor, 2vl, vla & vcl* Op.8. The Musikalischer Almanach of 1784 gives Berlin and Amsterdam as the place of publication of *Sechs Quarteten*, Op.8.

Op.9. *Six Sonatas for the Pianoforte, Harpsichord or Harp with Accompaniments for a Violin and Violoncello / Six Sonates pour le Violon avec la Basse Continue / Six Violin Solos*

The British Library has three versions of this composition dedicated to "Miss Ottley".

There are two copies of *Six Sonatas for the Pianoforte, Harpsichord or Harp with Accompaniments for a Violin and Violoncello* published by J. Welcker in London in 1775 in the British Library.[28]

There is also a 1780 French variant with an English title *Six Sonatas for Pianoforte, Harpsichord or Harp with Accompaniments for a Violin and Violoncello* published in London by J. Betz in 1780.[29] Longman & Broderip London catalogue for 1789 lists the composition as its own publication.

Among the Continental listings there is some confusion as to opus numbers. The sales catalogue of the Moffat Music Library gives *Six Sonates pour le Violon avec la Basse Continue* Op.9 published by B. Hummel in The Hague in 1765 which predates the Op.1 published in Britain. A B. Hummel 1775 edition of *Six Sonates pour le Violon avec la Basse Continue* is in the British Library. There is a note by Alfred Moffat on the endpaper saying that in 1922 he did not find a copy of this work in the British Museum. The note continues: "This is one of B. Hummel's early issues; probably about 1765." If the statement about the date were true, the work would have preceded Op.1. The title page, however, says

28 BL g .161.1.(5); h.2999.(2); R.M.26.c.1.(3)
29 BL h .1909.d

"Ouvre Neuvième".[30] A composition called *Solos a Violon et Basse* Op.9 is listed in the 1776 J. J. Hummel Hague catalogue.

The New Grove lists two under different names: *Six sonatas, vn, bc,* Op.9, 1775 in The Hague, *Six sonatas, pf/hpd/harp, vn, vc,* Op.9, 1776, in London. The Musikalischer Almanach gives The Hague as the place of publication of *Six Violin Solos,* Op.9.

Op.10. ***Six Overtures for Two Violins, Two Oboes or Flutes, Two French Horns, a Tenor and a Bass for the Harpsichord / Six Overtures for Two Violins, Two Oboes, or Flutes, Two French Hornes, a Tenor and a Bass for the Harpsichord / Six Sonates pour le Clavecin ou Pianoforte, avec l'Accompaniment d'un Violon et Violoncelle***

The British Library has one copy of this composition dedicated to "His Grace the Duke of Devonshire".

Six Overtures for Two Violins, Two Oboes or Flutes, Two French Horns, a Tenor and a Bass for the Harpsichord, was published in 1776 by P. Welcker in London.[31] There is doubt about the accuracy of this dating as P. Welcker died before 1776. It may have been published by his widow. The British Union List of Early Music and the New Grove date it as 1775. Another copy is at the Royal Academy of Music in London.

The Musikalischer Almanach lists two compositions as Op.10: *Six Overtures for Two Violins, Two Oboes, or Flutes, Two French Hornes, a Tenor and a Bass for the Harpsichord,* Op.10 published in London, and *Six Sonates pour le Clavecin ou Pianoforte, avec l'Accompaniment d'un Violon et Violoncelle* Op.10 published in Amsterdam. The 1772 catalogue of De la Chevardière, Paris offers as Op.10 *Sonates à violon seul.* The New Grove gives yet another title as Op.10: *Six sonatas, vn, b,* Op.10 published in Paris in 1772, while the 1776 catalogue of Hummel Hague has *Trios pour le clavecin* Op.10.

The term *Overtures* is used by Longman and Broderip, London in their 1781 catalogue.

---

[30] BL g .276.e
[31] BL g .474.a.(1)

Op.11. *Six Duettos for Two Violins*

The British Library has one copy of *Six Duettos for Two Violins* dedicated to "His Grace, The Duke of Dorset".

This work was engraved by J. B. Scherer and published by the author in c.1780. The title page states clearly, in Roman numerals, that it is Op.11.[32]

In the New Grove Op.11 is named as two compositions: *Concerto Violons*, Op.11 published in Paris c.1772, and *Six Duos, vn*, Op.11 published in Paris cca.1780. The catalogue of De la Chevardière Paris for 1772 lists *Concerto Violons* Op.11 among its publications. Hummel, The Hague offers in his catalogue of 1776 an *Overture* Op.11.

[A note about opus numbering:
Between Op.11 and Op.14 there is a clear gap in numbering. The numbering of Op.12 and Op.13 is therefore conjecture.]

Op.12. *Six Dancing Minuets in Three Parts for Two Violins and a Bass / Six Divertimentos, as Quartets, Three for Two Violins, a Tenor and Violoncello, and Three for a German flute or Hautboy, Two Violins and Violoncello / Duos pour Deux Violons / Concerto Violons*

The British Library has one copy of this composition dedicated to "The Selected Assembly at Newberry".

Six Dancing Minuets in Three Parts for Two Violins and a Bass without an opus number was published by J. Welcker in London in 1775.[33] Presumably it is the missing Op.12. Apart from the British Library it is at the Shakespeare Memorial Library. A later edition published by G. Walker in London in 1800 is at the Reid Library under the name of *Six Divertimentos, as Quartets, Three for Two Violins, a Tenor and Violoncello, and Three for a German flute or Hautboy, Two Violins and Violoncello* Op.12. The New Grove gives Op.12 as *Six Divertimentos*, a4, Op.12 published in London c.1790.

---

[32] BL g.218.ff (4)
[33] BL b.55.f

Longman and Broderip, London in their catalogues of 1778 and 1789 were offering Op.12 as *Quartets* Op.12. The composition is, however, a trio. The Musikalischer Almanach of 1784 gives Op.12 as *Sechs Violinduetten*, Op.12 published in Amsterdam. J. J. Hummel Hague in his 1781 catalogue gives Op.12 as *Duos pour Deux Violons* Op.12 published by himself in 1778. The 1772 catalogue of De la Chevardière, Paris offers as Op.12 *Concerto Violons* Op.12, presumably published by himself before 1772.

It is difficult to ascertain which the real Op.12 was. Was it a duet, a trio or a quartet, a concerto, or music written for a dance?

Op.13. - see [Various Op. Duets?] below

Op.14. *Six Divertimentos, Three for Two Violins a Tenor and Violoncello, and Three for a Hautboy or German Flute, Two violins and a Violoncello / Six Sonatas for Two Violin and Violoncello/ Six Quatuors pour Deux Violons Alto et Basse / Drei Quarteten für Flöte, 2 Violinen und Violoncell*

The British Library has two versions of this composition dedicated to "Sir Gregory Page Turner, Bart".

The composition, entitled *Six Divertimentos, Three for Two Violins a Tenor and Violoncello, and Three for a Hautboy or German Flute, Two violins and a Violoncello*, was published in 1780 by the composer himself.[34] It was printed by J. Caulfield. There are copies also at the Royal Academy of Music; London; and the London University Library.

The British Library also has *Six Quatuors pour Deux Violons Alto e Basse*, published by Sieber, Paris cca.1770.[35]

On the Continent there are two groups of quartets which may be the same work:

The 1774 catalogue of Sieber, Paris lists *Quatuors* published by Sieber. New Grove gives as Op.14. *Six quatuors, 2vn, va, b*, Op.14 published in Paris.

The Hummel Hague 1781 catalogue offers as Op.14 "Quartets Op.14"

---

[34] BL g.276.b
[35] BL h.1909.c

49

published by himself in 1781. Finally, the Musikalischer Almanach of 1784 gives *Drei Quarteten für Flöte, 2 Violinen und Violoncell*, Op.14 published in Berlin and Amsterdam.

[No Op.] *Six Divertimentos for the Harpsichord or Piano-Forte*

The British Library has one copy of this composition dedicated to "Lady Banks".

The *Six Divertimentos for the Harpsichord or Piano-Forte* was published by J. Preston in London.[36] The British Library catalogue gives the publication date as c.1783 and the opus number as 17, but the sales catalogue of the Moffat Music Library describes it as one of Preston's early publications and dates it as 1776. A note by Alfred Moffat on the end papers says that in 1927 the publication was not in the British Museum Library and that it was one of the early Preston publications.

Op.15. *Six Duetts, Four for Two Violins, and Two for a Violin and Tenor / Six Duos / Duos pour le Violin / Sechs Duetten für 2 Violinen, deren 2 für 1 Violine und eine Bratsche sind*

The British Library has one copy of this composition dedicated to "The Right Honourable, the Earl of Aylesford".

Six Duetts, Four for Two Violins, and Two for a Violin and Tenor was published by J. Preston in London in 1780[37] and again in 1785. The New Grove and the British Union Catalogue of Early Music dates it as 1785. There are copies in the Glasgow University Library and the Bodleian Library in Oxford.

As to the Continental version, the J. J. Hummel Hague catalogues lists it as *Six duos* Op.15 in 1781 and *Duos pour le violin* Op.17 in 1783, both published by J. J. Hummel in 1781. The opus number in the latter listing is wrong.

The Musikalischer Almanach lists it as *Sechs Duetten für 2 Violinen, deren 2 für 1 Violine und eine Bratsche sind,* Op.15, published in Berlin and Amsterdam.

----

[36] BL g .276.g
[37] BL g .218.(3)

Op.16. *Six Trios for Two Violins and a Violoncello, with a Thorough Bass for the Harpsichord / Six Sonatas for Two Violin and Violoncello / Six Trios à Deux Violons et Basse*

The British Library has two copies of this composition dedicated to "John Cochaine Sole, Esq.".

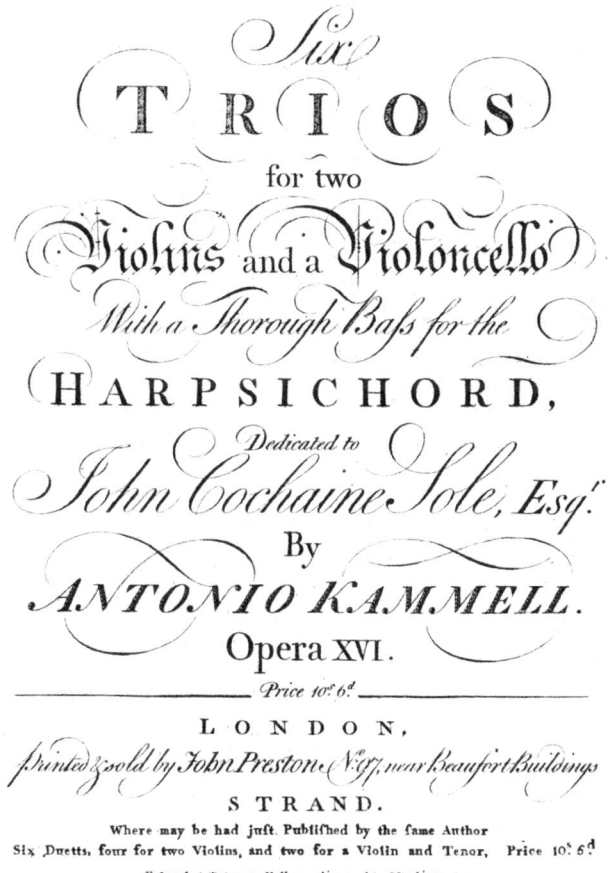

With a dedication John Cochaine Sole Esq., this title page of Opus 16 shows the John Preston of London publication

This composition, *Six Trios for Two Violins and a Violoncello, with a Thorough Bass for the Harpsichord*, was published by J. Preston in London in 1780[38] and again in 1785. Apart from the British Library it is at the Glasgow University Library and the Bodleian Library, Oxford.

The Hummel catalogue of 1781 lists it as *Trios à Deux Violons et Basse* Op.16 published in 1781. There is a copy of this edition entitled *Six Trios à Deux Violons et Basse* published c.1790 in the British Library.[39]

The New Grove lists two compositions as Op.16: *Six Sonates, hpd/pf, vn, vc*, Op.16 published in London c.1776, and *Six Sonates, 2vn, vc*, Op.16 published in London c.1785. The latter with the title *Six Sonatas for Two Violin and Violoncello* is in the British Library.[40]

Op.17. Six Divertimentos for a Violin and Tenor or Two Violins / Six Divertimentos pour Deux violons ou Violon et Alto Viola / Six quatuors ou Divertissements pour 2 Violons, Viola et Basse

The British Library has one copy of this composition dedicated to "Lady Banks".

Six Divertimentos for a Violin and Tenor or Two Violins, was published by J. Preston in London in 1781.[41]

The British Library lists another composition as Op.17 published c.1783 under the title *Six Divertimentos for the Harpsichord or Piano-Forte*. However, manuscript notes by Alfred Moffat suggest that it was an earlier work (see above between Op.14 and 15).[42]

There are various Continental listings which probably relate to this work: Sieber Paris catalogue 1776 *Simphonies* Op.17, De la Chevardière Paris catalogue 1777 *Trio Violons* Op.17, J. J. Hummel Hague catalogue 1781 *Six quatuors 3 for 2vl, vla, vcl; 3 for fl/ob, 2vl, vcl* Op.17 dated 1781. The British Union Catalogue of Early Music records a 1790 publication of *Six Divertimentos pour Deux violons ou Violon et Alto Viola*, Op.17 published by J. Schmidt in Amsterdam. There are copies in King's College Library in Cambridge and at the Royal Academy of Music in London. The

---

[38] BL g .411.(6); g.222.(12)
[39] BL g.420.c.(12)
[40] BL g .274.c.(1)
[41] BL h .219.a.(4)
[42] BL g .276.g

Musikalischer Almanach gives the place of publication of *Six quatuors ou Divertissements pour 2 Violons, Viola et Basse* Op.17 as Berlin and Amsterdam.

Op.18. *Six duettos for Two Violins / Six symphonies*

The British Library has one copy of this composition.[43]

Six duettos for Two Violins was published by the composer in 1782. It was engraved by T. Streight and sold at the Kerpen Music Shop. Apart from the British Library it is at the King's College Library, Cambridge. The sales catalogue of the Moffat Music Library dates it as c.1776.

The New Grove gives two titles for Op.18: *Six symphonies, 2vn, ve, b, 2ob, 2hn ad lib*, Op.18 published in Paris 1782 and *Six duettos, 2vn*, Op.18 published in London c.1785.

Op.19. *Six Notturnos for Two Violins and Violoncello / Six Violin Duetten*

The British Library has one copy of this composition dedicated to "Sir William Young, Bart".

Six Notturnos for Two Violins and Violoncello was published by the composer in 1784.[44] As the British Library copy is signed by him, it must have been published before his death in October of that year. There is also a copy in the King's College Library, Cambridge.

The British Union List of Early Music records another edition by J. Welcker c.1785 which is at the Reid Library in Edinburgh.

The New Grove lists two publications as Op.19: *Six Notturnos, 2vn, vc*, Op.19 published in London cca.1785 and *Six Duos, 2vn*, Op.19 published in Paris.

The Musikalischer Almanach 1784 lists it as *Six Violin Duetten*, Op.19 published in Paris.

---

[43] BL g .276.f
[44] BL g .276

Op.24. *Six duo concertants pour deux violons*

The British Library has one copy of this composition, published in Pars c.1785.[45]

[Note about opus numbering:
Op.24. is the last number for which a copy of the publication is available in the British Library. The opus numbers of compositions that follow are taken from secondary sources and are therefore not fully reliable.]

[Various Op. Nos.] Duets

None of these compositions is at the British Library.

Op.13 - another missing opus number - is listed four times in the Continental catalogues, each time with a different name: De la Chevardière Paris 1772 calls it *Concerto Violons* Op.13, Sieber Paris 1774 *Sonates* Op.13, the Musikalischer Almanach 1784 *Six Sonates a Violon avec Accomp. de Basse*, Op.13 published in Paris. The New Grove has Op.13 as *Six Sonates, vn, b*, Op.13 published in Paris.

Op.20 is given in the New Grove as *Six Duos, 2vn*, Op.20 published in Paris c.1777.

Op.22 is offered in the Sieber Paris catalogue of 1782 as *Duos* and listed in the New Grove as *Six duos, 2vn*, Op.22 published in Paris.

Op.26 is listed in the New Grove as *Six Duos, 2vn*, Op.26 published in Paris 1786.

There are also two unnumbered compositions in the New Grove under the titles *Six Duetti Notturni, 2vn* published in Paris c.1780, and *Six Duos Concertants, 2vn* published in Paris.

[Various Op. Nos.] Trios

None of these compositions is at the British Library.

---

[45] BL g.218.i.(8)

Op.23 is given in the New Grove as *Six Trios, 2vn*, Op.23 published in Paris 1782. This is presumably the same as the *Trios* Op.23 in the Sieber Paris 1782 catalogue.

Op.25 is given in the New Grove as *Six Notturnos, 2vn, b,* Op.25 published in Paris 1786. This is presumably the same as the *Trios* in the Sieber Paris 1786 catalogue.

Cover page of the Sieber of Paris publication of Six Trios, *Opus 23*

[Various Op. Nos.] Quartets

None of these compositions is in the British Library.

Op.21 is given in the New Grove as *Six Divertimentos, a4*, Op.21 published in 1777 in Paris. This is presumably the same as *Six Divertisement à Deux Violons, Alto et Violoncelle* Op.21 in the Sieber Paris 1778 catalogue.

Arrangements of Kammel's tunes during his lifetime

The catalogue of the British Library gives three collections of music arrangements using Kammel's tunes:

Musical Miscellany for the Harp or Harpsichord, edited by B. E. Jones and published in London c.1810[46], *A Second Collection of Airs and Marches for Two Violins, German Flutes and Hautboys, all of which have Basses for the Violoncello or Harpsichord* edited by Neil Stewart and published by N. Stewart in Edinburgh in 1770[47], *A Select Collection of French, English and Scotch Airs, taken from Compositions of the Most Approved Authors adapted for Two Violoncellos*, edited by James Blundell and published by Longman & Broderip in 1790.[48]

Twentieth century publications of Kammel's works

In the 1920s thanks to the interest of A. E. Moffat several of Kammel's works were published in Britain. Three were included in the series "Craxton-Moffat Coll. of Old Keyboard Music"[49] and published by J. B. Cramer in London: *Giga* in 1928, *Peasant dance* in 1928 and *Veaudeville* in 1933. Another, called *Serenade*, was published in *Morceaux du 18e siècle pour violon et piano* edited by A. E. Moffat and published in 1925 by Schott.[50] Apart from the British Library, the works *Giga* and *Peasant Dance* are also at the Sheffield University Library, *Vaudeville* at the library of Trinity College, Dublin.

Kammel's *Serenata in G* edited by Vratislav Bělský appeared in

---

[46] BL g .247.(2); R.M.16.d.18
[47] BL b.42.a
[48] BL h .1865.(2)
[49] BL g .1227
[50] BL h .1684.g.(2)

Serenate boeme, partite e notturni; in the series "Musica antiqua Bohemica" no.35 published by Artia Prague in 1958. It is at the London University Library and the Durham University Library. Another Czech publication was *Sonata [B flat major for violin and continuo]* in Tillinger R. *Houslové sonáty českého baroka*; Musica viva historica 18 published by Supraphon in Prague in 1967.[51]

In 1966 Chappell of London published Kammel's *Noturno* no.2 in *Music for Instrumental Ensemble* edited and arranged by T. J. Thompson & G. Eades.[52] Apart from the British Library it is also at the library of Trinity College, Dublin.

Sonata Op.10 no.2 was published in a collection *Böhmische Violinsonaten* edited by Sonja Gerlach and Zdeňka Pilková by G. Henle in Munich in 1982.[53] Apart from the British Library it is also at the Cambridge University Library.

A collection called *The Symphony 1720-1840 Series B; v.13* and published by Garland in London in 1884[54] contains two symphonies by Kammel edited by Zdeňka Pilková: *Symphony in D major* and *Symphony in G major*. The collection is also at the Aberdeen University Library, the Glasgow University Library and the Sheffield University Library.

Finally, *Divertimento Op.12 no.2 for Oboe or Flute (or Treble Recorder), Two Violins and Cello (or Bassoon), Divertimento Op.12 no.4 for Oboe or Flute (or Treble Recorder), two Violins and Cello (or Bassoon), and Divertimento Op.12 no.6 for Oboe or Flute (or Treble Recorder), two Violins and Cello* edited by C.M.M. and F. Nex were published by Phylloscopus Publications in Lancaster in 1993.[55]

Publishers, vendors, printers and engravers linked to Kammel's compositions

In the second half of the eighteenth century, publishing was closely related to printing and selling. The two were not independent activities.

The imprints of the period identified the printer and seller. Only in the

---

[51] BL g .818.1 18
[52] BL h .3210.j.(105)
[53] BL g .502.j.(1)
[54] BL g .1781/B13
[55] BL g .1373.g.(9);g.1373.g.(10);g.1373.g.(ll)

57

next century did they give the name of the publisher who neither printed nor sold the publication.

The names of people and places associated with the publication of Kammel's compositions during his lifetime, therefore, include printers, engravers, music shops and music publishers.

Much copying of music at that time was still done by hand. One purpose of printing music was to produce parts for performers quickly.

There was competition in the music market and a disregard of authors' and publishers' rights. Consequently the same composition was often issued simultaneously or in close succession by several publishers at home as well as abroad. Changing the imprint on the engraved title page was a simple matter and music notation did not present a language barrier. The result of these practices is a bibliographer's nightmare.

An entry in John Marsh's diary illustrates the point:

"...I got Preston find the paper and print off the copies I wanted, of which I desired some to be sent to Longman's in Cheapside for sale upon the usual terms, and as many to his partner Broderip in the Haymarket. Broderip might probably be displeased at my not employing them to engrave and print the work...".[56]

Brook describes the publishing piracy:

"Publishers like Artaria in Vienna, or Hummel in Holland, could, and did, re-engrave anything that had previously been printed in London or Paris, paying neither a farthing to the composer nor a florin to the original publisher".[57]

The parallel issues and reissues of Kammel's compositions were produced abroad in the Netherlands at the Hague and Amsterdam and in France in Paris.

A complete listing of publishers connected with Kammel is in Appendix III.

---

[56] Marsh, John (1998) p.348
[57] Brook, Barry S. "Piracy and Panacea in the dissemination of music in the late 18th century". In *Proceedings of the Royal Musical Association* vol.102, issue 1, 1975

Kammel's family and friends

Kammel's marriage and the Eddicatt family

In one of his early letters, Kammel wrote to Count Vincent Waldstein that he was hoping to marry a rich bride.[1] In the event, he married Ann Edicatt at St. Mary in St. Marylebone on 20 January 1768 and did not let the Count know. As she was a minor, the marriage had to be by licence with the consent of her father. She did not have much education and could not sign her own name. The choice of church suggests that Anthony and Ann's was not a "society" wedding.

Edicott and its variants Edicatt, Addicot, Endicott etc is a rare name. It is found mostly in the south-west (Cornwall, Devon, Somerset) and in London. Its origin appears to be French, with '-cot' being a corruption of the French '-court'. According to some researchers the Endicott line went back to John Yendecott, born in the first quarter of the 15th century, who was granted an estate on the edge of Dartmoor. The main seat of the West Country Endicott family had always been Middleton Manor at Chagford.

So far, no records have been found that would link Ann's father William Edicatt to the Cornish family. He was born sometime between 1715 and 1730 and married between 1740 and 1750 - either in London or in the West Country.[2]

Ann Edicout [sic] was baptized on 30 September 1750 at St. Anne's Soho. Her parents were William and Lydia. Their only other child to survive into adulthood was Lydia Edicotte baptized in 1756. Of their other children, one daughter Elizabeth Edicott baptized in 1767, died in childhood in 1770; no information is available about Joannah Edicott baptized in 1753, nor about William Edicutt baptized in 1762, and John Edicott baptized in 1765.

The father William Eddicatt, was buried at St. George Hanover Square on 16 September 1786. This suggests that he lived in Westminster, but the address is not known.

---

[1] Freemanová, Michaela (2001) p.18
[2] Some recorded births of William Edicatt (and variants) for the period: 12 November 1727 Throwleigh F. William M. Rebecca; 25 October 1724 Axminster F. William; 23 November 1718 Buckfastleigh Devon F. Nicholas; 19 September 1717 Abbotskerswell Devon F. Nicholas

It seems that by the time of the 1841 Census the London family had died out, since no Eddicats born and residing in London are listed.

Kammel's parish church, St. George, Hanover Square.
From engraving by T. Malton, 1787

The Besser Family

Lydia Eddicatt, the surviving younger sister of Kammel's wife Ann, married Charles Christian Besser at St. George Hanover Square 1 April 1783.[3] Weddings at this church in Westminster were considered important social events, indicating the bride and groom's social status. The match was probably arranged by Anthony Kammel who knew Besser from his business contacts. Charles Besser must have been close to Kammel, as he was later appointed executor of his Will.

Although the name Besser appears in Trowbridge and one christening is

---

[3] The licence for the marriage dated 31 March 1783 states that Charles Christian Besser was a 22 year old batchelor, residing at St. George Hanover Square. His occupation was "Merchant". According to the marriage register, the marriage record had a signature in the margin of "Faulckner of this parish". The Westminster Poll of 1774 gives three craftsmen of a similar name: Alexander Faulconer, cabinet maker in Whitcomb Street; Benjamin Faulkner, wine merchant in Blackmoor Street; and a Faulkener, chandler in Marsham Street. None of them was from St. George Hanover Square Parish.

recoded in Soho in 1745[4], Charles, noted in the Will as being "from Germany", seems to have returned there with his wife. He was not present during the probate of the Will, presumably because he was abroad.

St. George, Hanover Square, as it stands today.
Note roof extension to adjacent building

Kammel's children

Anne's first child, Lucy Cammell, was born 11 December 1769 and christened 31 December 1769 at Stratfield Saye, Hampshire. Kammel

---

[4] Elizabeth Sussanah Besser, daughter of Frederick and Mary Anne

was at the time away, giving concerts, and he must have taken his pregnant wife with him. As a result of this experience of giving birth away from home, Anne subsequently made sure that her other children were born in London. Lucy died in infancy and was buried on 9 July 1770 at St. Mary Le Bone. As Kammel had dedicated his first opus to Lucy Mann, he may have named his first child after her.

The remaining children were all baptized at St. George:

William born 4 November 1770, baptized 29 November 1770, not listed in Kammel's Will. Presumably he had died.

Elizabeth Rosina born 16 October 1772, baptized 30 November 1772. At the time of Kammel's death she was almost 12 years old.

Marcia Mary born 17 July 1774, baptized 29 July 1774. Her name, too, is not given in Kammel's Will. Presumably she had died.

George Anthony born 18 July 1775, baptized 2 September 1775. At the time of Kammel's death he was 9 years old.

Henry Christian John was born 27 November 1777, baptized 21 December 1777. At the time of Kammel's death he was almost 7 years old.

Horace Christopher born 27 February 1779, baptized 30 March 1779, not listed in Kammel's Will. Presumably he had died.

Henry James born 22 October 1780, baptized 12 November 1780. At the time of Kammel's death he was 3 years old.

There are a few more St. George burial records of children with a surname resembling that of Kammel:[5] Their baptism records are not available, but it seems unlikely that they were Anthony and Ann's children.

Kammel's death

In his Will signed 18 March 1784 he bequeathed to his wife Ann all

---

[5] Barnaby Cammell buried 1 January 1768; John Camell buried 10 May 1783 and Michael Camel buried 24 December 1780

household goods, plate and china and the sum of one hundred pounds. Among his effects, he did not list his violin.

To his daughter Elizabeth Rosina he gave three-hundred-pounds-worth of four percent Bank Annuities, to be transferred to her on her marriage, provided she married with the consent of her mother.

He directed his Executors to place his sons at the age of fourteen as apprentices to such trade as their mother and the Executors thought proper and to give them such sums they thought fit, not exceeding fifty pounds each.

The remainder was left to the Executors in a Trust, requiring them to pay the interest to his wife Ann for her own use during the rest of her natural life. After her death the residue was to be divided equally among his four children Elizabeth Rosina, George Anthony, John Christian and Henry or among those of them as would then be living.

The Executors were Charles Reeve of Half Moon Street, Charles Christian Besser of Germany, and Benjamin Starling of James Street Covent Garden.

The Will was signed in the presence of Thomas Reeve of Half Moon Street and William Lindeman of no.459 Strand.

The Will was proved on the 15 October 1784. The administration was granted to Charles Reeve and Benjamin Starling, two of the Executors named in the Will. Charles Besser was unable to attend.

The date of death is not given on the administrative copy of the Will. [6] The original Will, however, gives the date of his death in a marginal note as 5 October 1784.[7]

The circumstances of his death are not known, but considering that he died only six and a half months after signing his Will, it is safe to assume that his death was not unexpected.

There is a possibility that Anthony Kammel died at Norton Court in Kent during his stay as a guest of John C. Sole. On the 8 October 1784 there was a burial at St. Mary Norton of "George Kammell, Gent". The date of

---

6 PROB 11/1122 558, microfilm pp.312-3
7 PROB 10/2960

burial fits in between the date of death as noted on one of the copies of Anthony Kammel's Will and the proving of the Will.[8] The surname has the characteristic spelling of "K". The indication "Gent" suggests that he was an adult, which excludes the possibility of the funeral being that of his young son George who later (in 1788) became an apprentice. It also suggests that he had had some social standing. However, the first name is a puzzle. It could be a clerical error. Kammel was christened as "Johann Antonin" and signed his Will as "Anthony John". In the days of handwritten registers, mistakes were not uncommon.

Norton Court from the churchyard of St Mary Norton, Kent
Photo: ©Penny Mayes

The possibility of the buried person being Anthony Kammel is further strengthened by the fact that six years later his violin was offered in The Times for sale by auction of the effects of the late J. C. Sole.[9] Could

---

[8] The date of proving his Will was 15th October 1784, the date of death as noted on one of the copies of the Will [PROB10/2960] was 5th October 1784

[9] Six years after Kammell's death, the violin was offered in The Times for sale by auction: "Sales by Auction. By Mr. Greenwood at his room in Leicester Square, on Thursday 24th Inst. And following day at Eleven o'clock. A well chosen and valuable library of books, books of prints, and pictures, a capital violin which formerly belonged to the celebrated Kammel. Manuscript music never published, a two-feet telescope, several fine French, Carlo Marratt, and other burnished gold frames, and many other effects of J. C. Sole Esq. Brought from his seat, Norton Court, Kent. To be viewed to the Sale, and catalogues had." [*The Times* 22 June 1790, 25 June 1790]

Kammel, before he died, have actually given his violin to John C. Sole - either in gratitude and friendship or as payment of a debt?

There is another story about Kammel's violin told by his nephew Antonin Kammel.[10] He said that Kammel's old Cremona violin used to be in his Czech family till about the1870s, but that its present whereabouts were not known. This was unlikely to be the same violin as the one advertised for auction by Greenwood in London in 1790.

The church & graveyard of St Mary, Norton, Kent

Where did the Kammels live

On arrival in London, Kammel reported to Count Vincent Waldstein:

"I live thriftily in the company of Mr. Zappa, who is a very honest man".[11]

Zappa was a cellist who crossed the Channel on the same boat.

Other sources say that in the beginning Kammel was given hospitality by

---

[10] Mikanova, Eva (1989) p.139
[11] Freemanová, Michaela & Mikanová, Eva (2003b) p.211

Johann Christian Bach himself.[12]

Before his marriage in 1768 Kammel may have lived in Marylebone, as his marriage took place at St. Mary in Marylebone. On the other hand he may have lived, like many other musicians, in Soho.

A year later in 1769, the address where tickets for his concert could be obtained was given as the corner of Great Titchfield Street and Margaret Street near the Oxford Market. There is no evidence of Anthony Kammel living there, but the violinist John Crosdill did live in Titchfield Street. Perhaps Kammel lodged with him.

In May 1770, tickets for an Anthony Kammel concert were sold at Little Carrington Street, just round the corner from Half Moon Street where Kammel lived from 1770 or 1771. He moved to the house in 34 Half Moon Street, previously occupied by Lady Worgden, a few months after the death of his daughter Lucy in July 1770. The house is still standing today.[13]

In autumn 1785, about a year after Anthony's death, Ann Kammel left Half Moon Street and moved to 21 Kensington Gardens, a house previously occupied by Thomas Leadley. She paid rates for the whole half-year beginning March 1786 which suggests that she had no immediate plans to move. She moved out unexpectedly during the summer, and the property stood empty for a while before a new occupant moved in. She may have gone back to Westminster to look after her father.

Back in Half Moon Street a Mrs. Fuller moved into the house early in 1786.

Finally, by the end of the year, the house changed ownership from the Kammels to Donoghoe who, after the house had been standing empty for a few months, moved in during the spring of 1787.

We know neither where Ann Kammel was staying after leaving Kensington, nor where her father lived before his death.

---

[12] Mikanova, Eva (1989) p.141; Freemanová, Michaela & Mikanová, Eva (2003b) p.214
[13] Currently serving duty as part of the Hilton chain of hotels

Kammel's house at 34 Half Moon street, bordered by "Hilton International" flag and decorative lamp-post.

Kammel's friends and neighbours

When Anthony Kammel came to London he did not know many people. His friends were mostly musicians with whom he gave concerts, and people living nearby.

One of the early contacts he made was **Ann Elliott** of Greek Street. She was a witness to Anthony Kammel's marriage in 1768. Nothing more is known about her. She could have been Kammel's landlady before he married.

His closest friends were his neighbours **Charles & Thomas Reeve** of 32 Half Moon Street. Charles was described in a census as a "window tax collector, local dealer". In 1767 the rates for the house were paid by **William Reeve,** presumably Charles and Thomas's father. Thomas was a witness to Kammel's Will, Charles an executor. According to the Will, Charles with Kammel's wife shared the responsibility for choosing the trade for Kammel's sons and approving the groom of Kammel's daughter.

Other neighbours and friends from Half Moon Street were a physician **Michael Donaghoe**, a musician **Francis Hackwood, Lady Worgden** and **Mrs Fuller.**[14]

Two other people were associated with Kammel's Will: **William Lindeman** of 459 Strand who was a witness, and **Benjamin Starling** of James Street Covent Garden who was an executor.

Henry Noel was a witness to the marriage of Charles Besser and Lydia Edicatt in 1783. He was a relative of Lucy Mann. He could have been the "Mr. Nouelle" with whom Kammel travelled incognito in 1766.[15]

Charles Christian Besser, Kammel's brother-in-law from Germany, and executor of his Will, was very close to Kammel. However, we do not know how they first got to know each other. They may have met during Kammel's stay in Germany before his coming to England.

After Kammel's death the witnesses to Ann's 1787 marriage to Richard Tanner were **Edward & Milicent Hitchings** of St Marylebone. It is not clear whether they were friends of the Kammel or the Tanner family.

Kammel's business contacts:

Kammel, as was customary at the time, sold his published music and concert tickets from his home address. In addition he made use of London business contacts and music publishers listed in Appendix III.

---

[14] Michael Donaghoe moved to No.34 Half Moon Street in April 1784; Francis Hackwood lived in No.10 Half Moon Street between 1768-1781, in 1782 he moved to No.35 Half Moon Street, next door to Anthony Kammel; Lady Worgden is listed in the ratebooks under No.34 Half Moon Street before 1767; Mrs Fuller moved to No.34 Half Moon Street in February 1786.

[15] Freemanova, Michaela (2001) p.18

Outside of London Kammel was friends with **Benjamin Banks** (1727-1975), a violin maker in Salisbury. Kammel got to know him while taking part in the Salisbury Festivals. Blake's daughter Anne visited Kammel in London.[16]

Kammel's bank account at the Bank of England gives three names with whom Kammel must have had financial dealings:

John Hayward who paid £175 to Kammel on 30 May 1780. Between the years 1785 and 1796 John Howard was listed as a stock-broker in Oxford Street.

John Hoper paid Kammel £200 on 25 June 1778. John Hoper was vicar of Steyning, Head of the Steyning Grammar School and rector of Piccombe. There was also a builder called John Hooper who did some work for Kammel's friend Thomas Anson in Shugborough.

Thomas Stanton paid Kammel £200 on 5 August 1777. Since there were several people of this name at this time it is difficult to decide who he was and why he paid Kammel such a large sum.

Kammel's dedicatees and patrons

Kammel dedicated some of his compositions to various prominent people – either in gratitude for help received or in hope of support in the future. The wordings of the dedication on the title page ranged from a simple "for XY" to "humbly dedicated to XY by her grateful and most obedient humble servant". The words used in the dedication are an indicator of social distance between Kammel and the dedicatee, making it possible to divide the dedicatees into 5 groups.

In the first group are those whom Kammel considered fairly close to himself: "A select assembly at Newberry", George Pitt, John Cochrane Sole, Lady Lucy Mann.

A select assembly at Newberry: in the dedication of *Six Dancing Minuets* [without opus number] in 1775 does not mention any particular name, but it is connected with the Duke and Duchess of Devonshire (see below).

---

[16] Burrows, Donald & Dunhill, Rosemary (2001) p.1030

Lady Lucy Mann: Kammel's very first published composition *Sei Trii, di Violino e Basso* in 1766 was dedicated to her with the words: "La prima e la principale mia protettrice al mio comparire in questa capital (The first and main patron of mine to appear in that capital city)". Sir Horace Mann 1st Bt, a British representative in Florence, had a nephew also called Horatio Mann who became the 2nd Bt. The nephew married Lucy Noel in 1765 and had a daughter called Lucy christened 2 April 1766 in St. James West. Sir Horatio had his family seat at Bourne, near where possibly Kammel was buried. Within the grounds there was Sir Horatio's own Bishopsbourne Paddock cricket ground.

George Pitt (1721-1803): resided in Stratfield Saye where Kammel's daughter Lucy was born In 1769. In 1770 Kammel dedicated his *Six Quartettos for Two Violins a Tenor and Violoncello Obligato* Op.4 to George Pitt. Between 1761 and 1768 George Pitt was envoy to the Count of Turin. Did he meet Kammel in Italy?

John Cochrane Sole, to whom Kammel dedicated his *Six Trios for Two Violins and a Violoncello* Op.16 in 1780, was an educated man who lived at Havering Bower near Romford and later at North Court near Faversham. It is possible that Kammel was staying with him when he died and that he is buried in St. Mary Norton. After Sole's death his daughter auctioned his valuables, among them "a capital violin which formerly belonged to the celebrated Kammel".

In the second group are: Count Vincent Waldstein, the Duke of Devonshire and Miss Ottley.

Count Vincent Waldstein was Anthony Kammel's chief protector in his native country of Bohemia. Kammel dedicated his *A Second Sett of Six Sonatas for Two Violins and a Bass* Op.3 to him in 1769.

The **Duke of Devonshire**, William Cavendish, was the dedicatee of Kammel's *Six Overtures for Two Violins, Two Oboes or Flutes, Two French Horns, a Tenor and a Bass for the Harpsichord* Op.10 in 1776. The Duke was married to Georgiana née Spencer (see below).

Miss Ottley (for details of her family see below) had *Six Sonatas for the Pianoforte, Harpsichord or Harp with Accompaniments for a Violin and Violoncello* Op.9 dedicated to her in 1775.

In the third group are: Lady Banks, Sir Gregory Page Turner, the Earl of Aylesford.

Lady Banks, to whom Kammel dedicated his *Six Divertimentos for the Harpsichord or Pianoforte* [without opus number] in 1778 or earlier and his *Six Divertimentos for a Violin and Tenor or Two Violins* Op.17 in 1781. She was presumably Lady Dorothea Banks, wife of Sir Joseph Banks. The Bankses belonged to the Moravian Brethren Church. Kammel was not a member of the Church.[17] Sir Joseph Banks, whose sister was Sophia Sarah Banks, lived at 32 Soho Square and had a house in Kent called Provender very near to Norton Court, where Kammel is probably buried.[18]

The Earl of Aylesford, Heneage Finch, of Grosvenor Square. He was born in 1751 at Sion House, Isleworth, and died in 1821 at Gt. Packington in Warwickshire. In 1780 Kammel dedicated his *Six Duetts, Four for Two Violins, and Two for a Violin and Tenor* Op.15 to him.

Sir Gregory Page Turner, MP for Thirsk, of Portland Place was the dedicatee of Kammel's *Six Divertimentos, Three for Two Violins a Tenor and Violoncello, and Three for a Hautboy or German Flute* Op.14 in 1780. In the 1841 Census for St. Marylebone he is described as Independent and his birth given as about 1791.

His early 18th Century ancestor, Sir Gregory Page, second and last Baronet, spent a large part of his fortune on the purchase of the vast estate of Wricklemarch in Blackheath in 1725. He pulled down the old manor house and built what fifty years later was described as "the first habitable house in the Kingdom" at the cost of £90,000. He was childless and as such, on his death in 1775, bequeathed everything to his great-nephew Sir Gregory Turner who added Page to his surname.

In the fourth group are: Sir William Young, Lady Young of Delaford, the Countess Spencer, the Duke of Dorset.

Sir William Young was the dedicatee of Kammel's *Six Notturnos for Two Violins and Violoncello* Op.19 in 1784, and **Lady Young of Delaford** of Kammel's *Six Notturnos for Two Violins and a Bass* Op.6 in 1772. Sir William Young, 2nd Bt (1749-1815) was a Governor of Tobago and a politician. His country seat was Hartwell in Buckinghamshire. The Buckinghamshire archive has a "Map of the estate of Sir William Young, bart called Delaford, surveyed by John Bellingham in 1770".

---

[17] According to a letter from the Moravian library (17 September 1992)
[18] Heal, Ambrose. *London Tradesman's cards of the 18th century*. Batsford, 1925 p.27

The Countess Spencer and Duchess of Devonshire to whom Kammel dedicated his *A Second Sett of Six Quartettos for Two Violins a Tenor and Violoncello Obligato* Op.7 in 1775. In the same year Kammel dedicated his *Six Dancing Minuets* (without opus number) in 1775 to "a select assembly at Newberry". The Duchess used to visit her relative, Mr. Poyntz of Midgham House in Newberry. The archivist of Chatsworth House says that there is no mention of Kammel in the Chatsworth archive.

The Duke of Dorset had Kammel's *Six Duettos for Two Violins* dedicated to him in 1780. The 3rd Duke of Dorset was John Frederick Sackville. He died in 1799. He loved cricket as did his friend Horatio Mann. He was the owner of Knowle House at Knole near Sevenoaks in Kent.

And in the last group are: Thomas Anson and Richard Ottley.

Thomas Anson, MP for Litchfield, of St James Square. In 1770 Kammel dedicated his Op.5 *Six Duets for Two Violins* to him. He was elected 1761, married 1767, and died in 1773.

Kammel was composer in residence at his seat at Shugborough and performed at a series of Breakfast Concerts at Thomas Anson's London House, 15 St. James Square. James Harris of Salisbury (see below) wrote that the concerts featured "the best hands in London" and on Anson's death wrote: 'All his friends were sharers of his most elegant entertainments.' In his Will Anson left Anthony Kammel an annuity of £50.

Richard Ottley and **Miss Ottley** were dedicatees of Kammel's two compositions in 1775, *Six Solos for the Violin with a Thorough Bass for the Harpsichord* Op.8 and *Six Sonatas for the Pianoforte, Harpsichord or Harp with Accompaniments for a Violin and Violoncello* Op.9. Richard Ottley (1730-1775), the eldest son of Drewry Ottley, was born at St. Christophers, Dunstan Park, Thatcham, Berkshire, lived in Argyll Street, St. James Westminster. In 1770 he married Sarah Elizabeth Young at Iver, Buckinghamshire. He owned estates in St. Vincent and in Tobago. His son Drewry Ottley (1755-1805) was President and Chief Justice of St. Vincent. One of Drewry's sons was Sir Richard Ottley (1782-1845), born in St. Vincent, Chief Justice of Grenada in 1814 and later of Ceylon, knighted by King George IV at Carlton House on 22 March 1820.

Kammel's supporter who **did not have a composition dedicated to**

him, James Harris (1709-1780) was a philosopher and musical entrepreneur in Salisbury. He was a patron of Anthony Kammel and it was he who in his letters mentioned a whole series of concerts at 15 St. James Square where 'the best hands in London' (including Kammel) could be found.

Kammel and the British society

In the second half of the 18th century a large number of musicians lived in London. A directory published in 1794 lists more than 800 of them.[19] They lived mostly in Westminster – the largest number in Soho, a few rich ones in Mayfair and the not so successful ones in St. Marylebone.

Some, like Francesco Zappa, came to London just for a short stay, others, like Karl Friedrich Abel, settled in London for the rest of their lives, bringing with them their relations – in the case of Abel his mother and aunt - and even obtaining denization.[20]

Kammel's first contacts on arrival in London were the German musicians around Bach's son Johann Christian Bach. German musicians were attracted to London by their hope that Queen Charlotte would support their musical activities. Mrs. Papendiek, one of the Ladies in Waiting, writes about life in high society London. Kammel's name unfortunately does not figure in her descriptions.[21]

He also had three Kent friends with whom he shared the memory of his stay in Italy. They were not musicians themselves, but they supported him in his musical activity. They also offered him hospitality on their estates in Kent, where he used to go when he needed rest. One such trip is recorded in his correspondence with Count Vincent Waldstein as taking place in 1766 – the date when the first cricket match was held in Bourne. It would be interesting to know if a convalescing Anthony Kammel watched the match and if he shared his host's enthusiasm for the sport of cricket.[22]

---

[19] Doane J.: *A musical directory for the year 1794*. London: Westley 1794.
[20] Karl Friedrich Abel came to London in 1759. He lived with Bach in Meard Street, and later with Mr. Herve in Greek Street, in Carlisle Street, 201 Oxford Street and 6 Duke Street. His mother joined him in London where she died in 1766. He obtained denization 17 May 1775. After Bach's death he went to Germany, but returned to his house in Duke Street in 1785. He died in 1787
[21] Papendiek, Charlotte Louisa Henrietta (1887).
[22] Freemanova, Michaela (2001) p.18

It is curious that there is no record of any concerts by Kammel in Kent, although at the time there used to be some musical activity in Canterbury. Each year he travelled to play at various music festivals and in the houses of his rich music supporters. He also made a journey north up to Scotland as a travelling companion of one of his aristocratic friends. They both travelled incognito and we know only about the trip because he wrote about it to the Count Vincent Waldstein.

He must have been a good companion and was welcome in the houses of his wealthy friends. It is doubtful that he did any entertaining in his own house. It was not very big and he had little money. The house was primarily a family residence. It is likely that his wife Ann did not play any part in the social life of London, having had one child after another in quick succession. The only person whom he introduced to society was her younger sister Lydia. He promoted her musical career and found her a suitable husband.

There are indication that he liked women and the good life. In his letter to the Count there are comments about the beauty of women in the north. This does not mean that he was a philanderer. He felt his family responsibilities keenly.

In his musical life he was supported by his patrons. In everyday activities, he relied on a few practical friends from the business community, the Reeveses being among them. Little is known about his commercial efforts, selling wood from the Vincent Waldstein estate, except for a few of his letters to the Count. He was unsuccessful in this enterprise. He also made a loss, due to investing some of his money in the West Indies. Again, there are no sources which would throw more light on this.

His health was not very good and towards the end of his life it affected his concert playing. It is not clear what his illness was. Most likely he suffered from rheumatic arthritis which had always been rife among people in Britain. A few comments in his letters suggest that at times he also suffered from depression. We do not know how serious it was - it could have been due just to worry and overwork. On the other hand, at least one of his descendants suffered from a serious mental illness.

CHAPTER III

POST

POST

Kammel's descendants

Ann Kammel and the Tanner family

About a year after Anthony Kammel's death, in October 1785, his widow Ann moved to 21 Queens Gardens in Kensington. Living in Kensington was probably cheaper that in Mayfair and their house in Half Moon Street could be rented out. However, she did not stay in Kensington for long and left about July 1786. It is likely that she left in order to look after her father William Eddicat during his terminal illness. He died and was buried at St. George's Hanover Square on 16 September 1786.[1] The father's address at the time is not known, nor has any Will or Administration been found.

It was not easy for a widow with several children to manage on her own. A year later, on 12 December 1787, Ann Kammel married Richard Tanner at St. George's in Hanover Square.[2]

We cannot be sure who he was. The combination of the names Richard and Tanner was not a common one at the time, although there were quite a number of Tanner families in London, Rochester, Birmingham, Newbury and Surrey. They were mostly tradesmen and small businessmen. Marrying one was for Ann a step down the social scale.

Ann Kammel's second husband was most likely one of the Surrey Tanners from Warlingham. Richard and Mary Tanner in Surrey had eight children of whom Robert was the eldest and Richard, baptized in 1745, the youngest. Robert married Lydia and had a son Robert who was baptized in 1759 at St. Botolph in the City of London. It was probably he who later lived in Layton Street where Kammel's daughter (and Robert's step-cousin) Elizabeth Rosina lodged before her marriage. Richard married Hannah Knight and had a son Richard baptized in 1769 in Warlingham. Later, presumably as a widower, Richard married Ann Kammel.[3]

---

[1] William Edicatt buried 16 September 1786 St. George's HS [Westminster Archive]
[2] Richard Tanner x Ann Kammel 12 December 1787 St. George's HS [IGI]
[3] Richard Tanner ch. 16 June 1745 Warlingham Surrey f.Richard m.Mary [IGI]; Robert Tanner ch. 31 August 1728 in Warlingham Surrey f.Richard m.Mary[IGI]; Robert Tanner x Lydia Malin 2 December 1753 at St George Mayfair. [IGI]; Robert Tanner ch. 1 April 1759

It is unlikely that Richard and Ann had any children because Ann was too old. There is no information about the burial or the Will of Ann who may have predeceased him. Later, Richard may have re-married, though it is unlikely, or Ann may have re-married, but that is even less likely. There is a burial record for a Richard Tanner in 1819 in Shoreditch.[4]

We do not know where Richard and Ann lived. It is fairly certain that they moved away from Mayfair. Directories for the period do not give any records for Richard Tanner in the London area. They may have lived with one of the members of the wider Tanner family. Richard's burial record suggests that they may have lived in Shoreditch.

The Tanner family had many branches. In London, several London addresses are linked with them:

Rate books for 1791 and 1792 give the name Robert Tanner in Laystall Street. In 1793 - the year of the wedding of Ann's daughter Elizabeth Rosina – Robert's name in the rate book for this address is crossed out.[5] Had he died? Or had he handed the accommodation over to Elizabeth Rosina?

Between 1791 and 1793 William Tanner, Clock Engraver and Varnisher, had a house No.3 on the north side of Bear Alley.[6]

The Bunhill Fields Burial Ground records show that on 25 March 1800 there was a burial of Elizabeth Cammel, aged 26, brought from Banner Street. This person could not have been the same as Elizabeth Rosina who had married Edward William Gilbert in 1793.

St Botolph f.Robert m.Lydia [IGI]; Richard Tanner x Hannah Knight 27 October 1768 Warlingham [IGI]; Richard Tanner ch. 29 October 1769 Warlingham Surrey f, Richard m. Hannah Knight [IGI]
[4] A Richard Tanner aged 50 was buried in 1819 in St. Leonard Shoreditch. [London Burials Index]; ?Richard Tanner X Harriett Edser 20 September 1803 St Martin in the Fields. ?Charlotte Tanner ch. 9 September 1804 St. Martin in the Fields f Richard m. Harriet [IGI]
[5] Rt.Tanner Laystall St.East ["Rt" probably stands for Robert] [Camden Archive. Land Tax 1792, MR/PLT/2584]
[6] [Guildhall ms. 11316]

Kammel's children and their descendants

At the time of Kammel's death, four of his children were still alive: Elizabeth Rosina, George Anthony, Henry Christian John and Henry James.

The question is what happened to his eldest son **William**. When Anthony Kammel signed his Will, William would have been almost 14 years old. It is possible that he was not mentioned in the Will because he did not need any money for his apprenticeship - he had been apprenticed already. So far no information about his trade or business has been found.[7] On the other hand, he may have died in childhood.

Elizabeth Rosina Gilbert and the Gilbert family

Elizabeth Rosina was born on 16 October 1772 and baptized on 30 November 1772. In 1788 she became apprenticed with Elizabeth Harris as a childs coat maker.[8] At the time of Anthony Kammel's death she was almost 12 years old. According to his Will she was due to receive £300 on marriage. Anthony Kammel's account at the Bank of England closed on 23 July 1793 with the transfer of £300 to E. R. Gilbert - her married name.

On 6 July 1793 at the age of 21 she married Edward William Gilbert at St. George the Martyr in Queen Square by licence.[9]

One of the witnesses to the wedding, Mary Daniells, was from Egham and had probably known Edward William since childhood. This confirms

---

[7] However, in the St. George the Martyr rate books for 1796 and 1797 under Brownlow Street there is an entry for "William Kamm" [Camden Arch.]
[8] UK Register of Duties Paid for Apprentices' Indentures, 1710-1811
[9] The text of the licence reads: "Licence dated 5 July 1793. Appeared personally Edward William Gilbert and made Oath, that he is of the Parish of St. George the Martyr in the county of Middlesex Batchelor aged twenty one years and upwards and intendeth to marry with Elizabeth Rosina Kammel of the parish of St. George the Martyr aforsaid Spinster aged twenty one years and upwards and that he knoweth of no lawful impediments to solemnize the same in the parish of St. George the Martyr aforsaid and further made Oath that the usual place of Abode of him the said Edward William Gilbert hath been in the said Parish of St. George the Martyr for the Space of four Weeks last past. E. W. Gilbert. Sworn before me Geo. Harris Surrogate"; The marriage register says: "St. George the Martyr Queen Street 1793 No.484 [X096/231]. Edward William Gilbert of this Parish and Elizabeth Rosina Kammel of the same Parish Married in this church by Licence this Sixth day of July in the year 1793 by me I. Brill [signed by both]. In the presence of Susannah Goromell, Mary Daniels."

which Gilbert family Edward William came from. The name of the other witness is illegible.[10]

Edward William was born 1772 in Egham, Surrey, his father was Edward, his mother Elizabeth. So much is certain. The rest is hypothesis:[11]

The Gilbert family had businesses or properties at St. Olave, Southwark, Egham and Staines in Surrey, and in Gosport and its vicinity in Hampshire.

In 1799 Elizabeth Rosina was widowed when Edward William died. The burial register of St. George the Martyr gives the date of Edward Gilbert's burial as 17 March 1799. His address is given as Devonshire Street, Queen Square. This is the address of Edward Gilbert, a japanner whose Will was signed by him on 7 February 1799 and proved on 14 February 1799. The witnesses to the Will were: Benjamin Winter and John Brooks.[12] The dates suggest that his death was sudden.

---

[10] Mary Daniells ch.19 November 1769 Egham Surrey f.William m.Ann [IGI].William Daniel x Anne Segery 17 November 1754 Egham, Surrey; The second witness could have been Susannah Hall Cornwall, London Mddx - her Will PROB11/2173 1843

[11] His grandfather was Joseph, son of Thomas and Mary (or Anne). He was born in 1706 in Rugeley and married Elizabeth Osborn in 1726 in Lichfield, Staffs. He was a shipwright by trade, and died some time before 1781. His daughter Mary was born in 1726 in Gosport and married Jonathan Mason at Fareham near Gosport in 1758. His son William was born 1727 in Gosport. Another son Edward, who was to be Edward Williams's father, was born 1737 at Alverstoke. In 1753 Edward was apprenticed as ironmonger and by 1761 had his own shop in Staines. In 1764 he married Elizabeth in Esher. He died some time before 1786. In 1786 Elizabeth wrote her Will, she died in 1790. They had three children. The eldest was probably Thomas, mentioned in the 1781 Will of his great-uncle Thomas Gilbert of Gosport. Nothing else is known about him. He might have married in 1789, either Ann Tilleard in St. Ann Soho or Hannah Eltham in Kingston or Sarah Beckford in Richmond. The youngest child was Emelia mentioned in her mother's Will of 1786 as being under 21. There is no trace of the birth register entry. Edward William was probably the middle child, born in 1772. Little is known about him. It is not surprising that he was not mentioned in the Wills of his great uncles and aunts written before his birth: Matthew's in 1762, Edward's in 1764, Mary's in 1766, Susan's in 1770. There were, however, two Wills written after his birth which also did not mention him: Thomas's in 1781 and Elizabeth's in 1786

[12] Benjamin Winter was baptized 1 December 1742 in Mortlake, he married Mary Elcock 11 August 1772 at St. Anne Soho. Their son Benjamin was baptized 2 April 1775 at St. Anne Soho and married Mary Whitman in 1797 in St. Marylebone. [IGI] The Will index at the Genealogcal Society gives the date of Benjamin Winter sr. as June 1790, but the Documents Online do not have such a will.

No records have been found of his apprenticeship as a japanner or of his having had a business. By a coincidence, however, Elizabeth Rosina's brother was also a japanner.

The children and descendants of Edward William and Elizabeth Rosina Gilbert:

Elizabeth Rosina's first child was **Edward George Antonio Gilbert** baptized in 1794 at St. Dunstan in the West. He probably married Tabitha Hosier at St. Dunstan in 1824. In 1841 they lived at Newington, together with their children born in Surrey: Tabitha in 1826, Edward in 1824 and Matilda 1832. The father, Edward, was a clerk and must have died before 1851. The head of the family in the 1851 Census was Tabitha Gilbert who lived at 78 Great Dover Street, Newington together with her unmarried son Edward. His occupation was "Professor of Music". In 1861 she lived in Isleworth with her daughter Tabitha. She died in Holborn in 1870, probably while living with her son.[13]

Edward's daughter **Tabitha Limpus** married in 1848 Richard Limpus, an organist in Newington. By 1861 they moved to Isleworth and by 1871 to Holborn where Richard died in 1875. The widow Tabitha is described in the 1881 census as teacher of music. She died in 1889. They did not have any children.[14]

Edward's daughter **Matilda Snosswell,** later Wesley, married in 1866 William T. Snosswell. He was retired and lived on annuity. When he died she married civil engineer Mathias Erasmus Wesley in 1879. They lived in 4 Norland Place, Kensington. She died in Kensington in 1907. She did not have any children from either marriage.[15]

---

[13] Edward George Antonio Gilbert ch. 28 May 1794 St. Dunstan in the West [IGI]; Edward Gilbert x Tabitha Hosier 8 January 1824 St. Dunstan, Stepney [IGI]; 1841 Census Ann's Place, St. Mary Newington; 1851 Census 78 Great Dover Street, Newington; Tabitha Gilbert died at 74 Holborn v.1b p.424 July-September 1870 [Freebmd]
[14] Richard Lumpus x Tabitha Ann Gilbert in Camberwell v,4 p.48 July-September 1848 [Freebmd]; 1851 Census: organist at 7 Webbs County Terrace, New Kent Road , Newington; 1861 Census: Musician, Elizabeth Cottages, Mill Platt, Isleworth; 1871 Census: organist at Queen Square St. George the Martyr; Richard David Limpus died at the age of 50 Holborn v.1b p.471 January-March 1875 [Freebmd]; 1881 Census: Tabitha A. Limfas, widow, teacher of music, at 95 Great Russell Street, St. Giles in the Fields; Limpus Tabitha Ann died at 63 St. Giles v.1b p.380 January-March 1889 [Freebmd]
[15] Snoswell, William T. x Matilda Mary Gilbert, Whitechapel 1c 65 7 March 1866 [Freebmd]; Wesley Matilda Mary died 76 Kensington 1a 8 2 December 1907 [Freebmd].

Edward's son **Edward Gilbert** was listed in the 1861 Census as an "unmarried" musical professor living in Camberwell. He must have married soon after and moved to Penge. His wife was Caroline Mary Sale whom he married in Pancras in 1866. His son Newton Edward Sale Gilbert was born in 1868 and his second son Erasmus James Denby Gilbert in 1869. By 1871 he had moved to Holborn where his small sons were looked after by a French nurse. His wife died in 1870 and he ten years later.[16]

Edward's grandsons **Newton Edward Sale Gilbert** and **Erasmus James Denby Gilbert** were born in Penge. They were sent to a boarding school in Margate. By 1891 Newton was an accountants articled clerk and Erasmus was a solicitor. They lived together as boarders in Camberwell. In the 1901 Census Newton's initials are listed among the certified patients at the Warmford Lunatic Asylum in Headington where he died in 1916. There is no information about Erasmus in 1901, in 1911 he was retired through illness and living on private means in Brighton. He died in Steyning in 1923. Neither of them was married and they did not have any children.[17]

Elizabeth Rosina's second child may have been **Thomas Gilbert** whose 1795 baptism is recorded in the Parish of St. George's Hanover Square. His parents' names are given as Edward (not Edward William) and Elizabeth. Did she perhaps have her first child baptized at the church where she had been baptized herself? Little is known about him. In the 1841 Census there was a silk weaver in Stepney called Thomas Gilbert and born 1794. There is also a tailor called Thomas Gilbert born 1796 who lived in the vicinity of St. George's Hanover Square. By 1851 the silk weaver had moved to Bethnal Green, while the tailor is not listed. I think it unlikely that either of them was Elizabeth Rosina's child. [18]

---

[16] 1861 Census: 3 Surrey Terrace Camberwell; Caroline M. Sale x Edward Gilbert Pancras v.1b p.11 September 1866 [Freebmd]; Caroline Mary Sale Derby v.19 p.429 September 1838 [Freebmd]; 1871 census Lt Queen Square, St. George the Martyr; Caroline Mary Gilbert Holborn v.1b p.420 September 1870 [Freebmd]; Edward Gilbert died at 56 St. Giles v.1b p.368 July-September 1880 [Freebmd]

[17] Newton Edward Sale Gilbert Croydon v.2a p.199 June 1868; 1881 Census: Lausanne House Schl, Addington St., Margate; 1891 Census: 45 The Gardens, Camberwell; 1901 and 1911 Census: Warmford Lunatic Asylum, St. Clement, Oxford; died aged 48 Hedington v.3a p.1100 June 1916; Erasmus James Denby Gilbert Croydon v.21 p.209 June 1869 [Freebmd]; 1881 Census: Lausanne House Schl, Addington St., Margate; 1891 Census: 45 The Gardens, Camberwell; 1901 Census:NIL; 1911 Census: 6 St. Georges Terrace, Brighton; died aged 57 Steyning v.2b p.337 December 1923 [Freebmd]

[18] Census 1841: Hobson Place Stepney; Census 1841: Mount Street, St. George Hanover Square; Thomas Gilbert died Westminster v.1 p.412 March 1851 [Freebmd]

In 1799, the year when her husband died, Elizabeth Rosina's third child **Joseph Gilbert** was baptized at St. George the Martyr in Holborn. Nothing of certainty is known about his life. There is a 1824 marriage record of a widower, Josef Gilbert and a widow, Rebecca Shambrook in Southwark which could be his. There is no record of any children born to this couple. Their names do not appear in the 1841, 1851 and 1861 Census.[19]

Where did Edward William and Elizabeth Rosina Gilbert live?:
Before her wedding, Elizabeth Rosina lived probably in Laystall Street Holborn, in Robert Tanner's household.[20]

According to the marriage licence, Edward William Gilbert was also "of this Parish". The only Gilbert listed in the rate books of the parish between 1791 and 1795 lived in Johns Mews. In 1796 his name at that address was replaced by Green.[21] Edward William could by then have lived with Sarah Gilbert in Gt. Ormond Street.

In the St. Andrew Parish Holborn lived a Thomas Gilbert who may have been Edward's elder brother, and his wife Ann. Their son Edward Charles Gilbert was baptized in 1796.[22]

In 1795-1796 the Gilberts first shared house with George and then James Abbott in Bedford Street which adjoins Laystall Street.[23] In 1797 their name was crossed out.

It is possible that the Gilberts moved to Devonshire Street.[24]

---

[19] [LMA x096/229; x102/051]; Joseph Gilbert X Rebecca Shambrook 31 October 1824 St. George the Martyr Southwark [IGI]. Joseph was a widower, Rebecca a window, their witness was Eliza Shambrook.
[20] St. Andrew Holborn & St. George the Martyr. Poor Rate 1791 [Camden Arch]
[21] St. Andrew Holborn & St George the Martyr. Poor Rate 1791-1796 [Camden Arch]
[22] Thomas Gilbert married Ann Tilleard 30 July 1789 in St. Anne Soho.[IGI]; There is no marriage recorded for Edward Charles Gilbert; his name is not in the censuses 1841, 1861 or 1871.
[23] PROB 11/1310 James Abbott 24 August 1798 Oilman of Bedford Street, wife Elizabeth; Witnesses: Joseph Bayley & William Bennet
[24] According to the rate books for between 1791 and 1795 there was no Gilbert in Devonshire Street, Holborn. In 1797 Edward Gilbert's name was listed in Devonshire Street with a note "from Xmas". It replaced the name of Sarah Harrison. Gilbert's name was listed again in 1798. In the rate book for 1799 the name of Edward Gilbert in Devonshire Street was crossed out and the name of Sarah Gilbert's substituted. [Camden Arch]

A year after Edward William's death, in the rate book for 1800, the only Gilbert in Devonshire Street was Sarah. She was probably Edward's cousin who had previously lived in Gt. Ormond Street.[25]

Elizabeth Rosina Brown and the Brown family

Five years after being widowed, Elizabeth Rosina married James Brown at St. George's Hanover Square on 28 October 1804. Their licence was issued as early as 20 April 1804. Why the delay of six months?

James Brown was described as a bachelor "of the Parish of St. James Westminster" and she as a widow "of the Parish" (i.e. St. George's Hanover Square). They both signed the register which means that she was literate. Their witnesses were P. Didier and Catherine Loriot - both names possibly Huegenot origin. Loriot was a St. James family.[26] In 1841 Edward Loriot lived in Albany Road in Camberwell – the same road where James Brown probably died in 1833. This suggests a long term friendship between James Brown and the Loriot family.

James Brown's identity is something of a mystery because his name is so common.

He may have been the son of a Huegenot couple, baptized as Jacques Brown on 14 March 1784.[27]

---

[25] [Land Tax 1794] Sarah Gilbert Gt. Ormond Street South [MR/PLT/2588] [Utah35 Poor Rate 1791-1800] Sarah Gilbert in Gt. Ormond Street in 1791, 1792, 1793. 1795, 1796. In 1797, 1798, her house is empty. In 1799 her name replaces that of Edward Gilbert in Devonshire Street. In 1800 her name is listed in Devonshire Street. [Camden Arch]; PROB11/2043Will of Sarah Gilbert: Written 14 November 1845 probate 9 November 1846: To nieces and nephew: Sarah Fford, Ann Sams nee Fford wife of John Sams of Chapel Street, St. Leonard, Mary Fford, Elizabeth Suthers nee Fford wife of William Suthers - children of brother William; Edward William Gilbert had cousins Mary (b.1761), Sarah (b.1774) and William (b.1766) - children of his uncle William (b.1726). Mary Gilbert's name replaced that of Moritmer in Gt. Ormond Street a few houses away from Sarah in 1796. In fact, Mary's name was entered twice in the street suggesting perhaps that she had two houses. Her name appeared twice each year for 1797, 1798. [Camden Arch]

[26] Peter Didier married Sara Tebbet 13 January 1801 at St. George's Hanover Square. Their witnesses were Thomas Rowley and Sarah Didier. [West Arch]; Mary Louisa Loriot was baptized 29 April 1790 at St. James's. Her father was Edward, mother Mary [IGI]. There is no Catherine Loriot in IGI.

[27] Jaques Brown born 24 February 1784 baptized 14 March 1784 Threadneedle Hugenot f.Jaques m. Ann Elizabeth Baudouin, P. Jaquaes David Baudouin, M. Catherine Bauduoin. [IGI]

84

Years later, in Elisabeth Rosina Brown's death certificate, her late husband's occupation was given as "Clerk in the Office of the late Duke of York". However, there is no mention of him in the Royal Kalendar for the period and the Royal Archive at Windsor has no information about the Duke of York employees.[28]

The Browns lived in Green Street, now Rushworth Street, Southwark where their daughter Elizabeth Brown was born 18 February 1807. They probably owned several properties and sublet them to tenants. Later as a widow Elizabeth Rosina probably had an independent income from them.

James Brown and his family may have moved around with his work for the Duke of York. We do not know what employment he had after the Duke of York's death.

He may have died in Southwark in 1833.[29]

Elizabeth Rosina Brown died at Cheam on 14 June 1846 after 6 months' lung illness and fever. The death was reported by her daughter Elizabeth Baker who was present.[30]

It is not known where Elizabeth Rosina had lived immediately before her death.

In the 1841 Census there is an Elizabeth Brown, aged 75, independent, not born in Surrey, living in High Street, Cheam. The head of the household was Thomas Cusden, 75, independent, born in Surrey. Her age does not fully match the census record, however.

There are two other persons with the same name listed in the 1841 Census at Southwark:

---

[28] Frederick Augustus, the Duke of York and Albany (16 August 1763 - 5 January 1827), second son of George III, Commander in Chief 3 April 1778, resigned 25 March 1809, reappointed 29 May 1811 until his death

[29] James Brown buried 15 May 1833 St. George Southwark, address at death: Albany Place East Lane. [City of London Burials]. The name Albany Place was replaced in 1862 by Albany Road. The Soutwark librarian says that properties in East Lane were let to tenants by Brown.

[30] The death certificate gives her name as Elizabeth Rosanne. Epsom vol.4.p.92 April-June 1846 [Freebmd]

Elizabeth Brown, aged 65, not born in Surrey, living in Alfred Place, St. George the Martyr. Alfred Place is very near to Green Street where the Browns used to live; and Elizabeth Brown, aged 70, not born in Surrey, living in George Street, St. George the Martyr.

The children and descendants of James and Elizabeth Rosina Brown:

Although in her second marriage Elisabeth Rosina was getting on in years, she bore several children in Southwark.

Elizabeth Rosina Brown's fourth child, **James Henry Brown**, was baptized in 1805 at St. George the Martyr Southwark. There are two possible records of his marriage: He either married Sarah in the City or Mary in Southwark or maybe he did not marry at all.[31]

Elizabeth Rosina Brown's fifth child was **Elizabeth Brown** born at Southwark in 1806 and baptized a month later in 1807 who died in infancy and another child was later given the name Elizabeth.[32]

Elizabeth Rosina Brown's sixth child, **Mary Brown**, was born at Southwark in 1808 and baptized in 1809.[33] There is no further information about her.

In 1809 Elizabeth Rosina Brown gave birth to her seventh child and called her **Eliza Brown**.[34]

Elizabeth Rosina Brown's daughter, **Elizabeth Brown**, baptized at Southwark in 1809, married James Dixon Baker at St. Mary Newington in 1831.

Elizabeth Baker died 1887 aged 79 in Powder Mills Cottages. Her husband James Baker had been a labourer at Powder Mill. According to

---

[31] James Henry Brown ch. 27 January 1805 St. George the Martyr Southwark [IGI]; James Henry Brown x Sarah Elizabeth Mills at St. Vedast in the City 4 August 1829; [IGI]; 1841 Census James Brown, Mary Brown, Charles Street, Charles Court, St. George the Martyr, Sarah b.1837, James b.1841 – father not born in Surrey, not Henry either

[32] Elizabeth Brown ch.18 February 1807 St. George the Martyr Southwark, Green Street now Rushworth Street.

[33] Mary Brown, b. 17 November 1807, ch.7 December 1808 St. George the Martyr Southwark. [IGI].

[34] Eliza Brown ch.11 June 1809 St. George the Martyr Southwark [IGI]

86

the 1891 Census, he was blind and after his wife's death was looked after by his daughter Sarah. He died in 1895 at Court Cottages, his daughter was present at his death.

They had nine children, all of them born in Ewell: **James Baker** born about 1831, **John Baker** 1833, **Rachel Baker** 1835, **Thomas Simms Baker** 1837, **George Baker** 1839, **Eliza Baker** 1841, **William Charles Baker** 1845, **Mary Ann Baker** 1847, **Sarah Ann Baker** 1854.

It is possible that Elizabeth Rosina Brown had three more children, though she would have been rather old. The three - all of them born in Southwark - were: **Amey Brown** born in 1811, **Harriet Brown** in 1813 and **John Brown** in 1816.[35]

The Children and descendants of James and Elizabeth Baker[36]

Elizabeth Rosina Brown's grandchild and Elizabeth Baker's first child, **James Baker**, born about 1831, lived in 1840s and 1850s with his parents in the Marsh at Ewell where there was a powder factory. In 1861 he and his wife Ann Baker, five years younger than him, lived at Ewell Lower Marsh. He was a "powder maker". He died in an explosion in 1863. After his death, his wife married a John Godfrey. Their children, all born in Ewell, were: **Louisa Baker** about 1852, **James Joseph Baker** about 1854, **Thomas Baker** about 1856, **John Baker** about 1858, **Robert Baker** about 1860 and **William James Baker** about 1863.

Elizabeth Baker's grandchild and James Baker's first child, **Louisa Baker,** was born in 1852. In 1861 she lived with her parents, in 1871 she was a domestic servant in Upper Marsh. In 1875 she married Thomas Ditch in 1875. They had eight children: **Lucy Agnes Ditch** 1876, **Caroline Sarah Ditch** 1880, **Thomas Ditch** 1882, **Charles Ditch** 1885, **Joseph John**, also known as **Topher Ditch** 1886, **Leonora Ditch** 1888, **Clara Ditch** 1891, **Elizabeth Ditch** 1893. Their father Thomas died probably in 1922, their mother must have died sometime before 1911.

---

[35] Amey Brown ch. 15 November 1811 St. Saviour [IGI]; Harriet Brown ch. 14 July 1813 St. George the Martyr [IGI]; John Brown ch. 28 August 1816 St. George the Martyr [IGI]
[36] Information taken from Census 1841, 1851, 1861, 1871, 1881, 1891, 1901, 1911 and from Freebmd

Elizabeth Baker's grandchild and James Baker's second child, **James Baker**, was born in 1853. He lived with both parents in 1861. In the 1871 Census his mother's surname was Bidwell - presumably she remarried after becoming a widow. He was a carpenter. By 1881 he lived in Newington with wife Mary. He died in Ewell in1917.

Elizabeth Baker's grandchild and James Baker's third child, **Thomas Baker**, was born in 1855. In 1861 he lived with his parents, in 1871 he was a carpenter in Upper Marsh.

Elizabeth Baker's grandchild and James Baker's fourth child, **John Baker**, was born in 1857. In 1861 he lived with his parents, in 1871 he was a general servant at the Wheat Sheaf public house in Ewell, and then in 1881 a groom and domestic servant at the Stable Yard, Hatchford Estate at Cobham.

Elizabeth Baker's grandchild and James Baker's fifth child Robert Baker was born in 1860.

Elizabeth Baker's grandchild and James Baker's sixth child William James Baker was born about 1863.

Elizabeth Baker's second child, **John Baker**, was baptized in1833 at Ewell and buried 1841 in Epsom.

Elizabeth Baker's third child, **Rachel Baker**, was baptized in 1835 at Ewell. She lived with her parents in 1851, but not in 1861. She must either have left home or died.

Elizabeth Baker's fourth child, **Thomas Simms Baker**, was born in 1837. He lived with his parents in 1851, but not in 1861. In 1869 he was a Corporal in the 3rd Hussars.

Elizabeth Baker's fifth child, **George Baker**, born in1839, was a brick maker in Kingston in 1861.

Elizabeth Baker's sixth child, **Eliza Baker**, born in 1841, married Robert Chandler in 1872 at Albury, Surrey. On the death of her sister Sarah Ann Baker, she inherited £41.

Eliza Chandler had ten children, all but the first one born at Hambledon, Surrey: **Henry Chandler** born in 1873, **Louisa Jane Chandler** born in 1874, **William Alfred Chandler** born in 1876, **Rosa Chandler** born in

1878, **Lily Chandler** born in 1878, **Annie Chandler** born about 1880, **Ethel Chandler** born in 1883, **Eliza Chandler** born in 1885, **Minnie Chandler** born in 1886, **Robert Chandler** born about 1891.

In 1842 her address was 1 Rosebery Terrace, West Ewell.

In 1891 they lived in Snowdenham Road, Bramley, Surrey. Her husband was a "sawyer". In 1901 only their youngest son, **Robert T. Chandler**, and one grandson, **Albert Chandler**, lived with them. By 1911 she was a widow and lived with her 20 year old son who was a gardener, and her 14 year old grandson who was a printer's boy, at Sunbury Lane at Walton on Thames.

Elizabeth Baker's seventh child, **William Charles Baker**, was born in 1845. He lived at his parents' in Ewell in the 1850s and 1860s. He was an "agricultural labourer". By 1871 he lived at Bennetts Cottage, Hanworth with his wife called Emma Ann Baker born in 1845 and three of his wife's siblings: her sister Eliza Penfold born about 1858, and her brothers Thomas Penfold born about 1855 and William Simon Penfold born about 1866. In 1881 they all lived at Laburnum Cottages, Hanworth. Emma Ann Baker died in Staines in late 1881. Her sister Mary Ann Penfold went away to marry Charles Thomas in 1882. When he died, she returned and married her late sister's widower William Charles Baker in December 1890. The following year they lived in Church Road, Mitcham, together with Mary Ann's two children from her previous marriage: Charles F. Thomas born about 1883 and George Peter Thomas born about 1881. By then William Charles Baker's occupation was "varnish maker". In 1901 he and his wife Mary Ann lived in Homewood Road, Mitcham. They had one son **Albert Edward Baker** born at Mitcham about 1896. Mary Ann's son from her previous marriage, George Peter Thomas, lived with them. He was a "general labourer". In 1907 Mary Ann died and by 1911 William Charles was living with his third wife Hannah Baker, born about 1851, in 24 Broomfield Road, Tolworth. His son Albert Edward Baker was an "iron monger assistant".

Elizabeth Baker's eighth child, **Mary Ann Baker**, was baptized in 1847 at Ewell. She lived with her parents in 1851, but not in 1861. She must either have left home or died.

Elizabeth Baker's ninth child, **Sarah Ann Baker**, was born in 1854. She lived with her parents in 1851, but not in 1861. In 1871 she was a servant in the household of a general medical practitioner. In 1881 she lived with her parents again at the Late Powder Mills, her occupation was given as "domestic servant". By 1891 her mother was dead and her father blind. She was looking after him. She was present at the death of both her mother and her father. She herself died at Ewell Court Lodge in 1898 where she was a "lodge keeper". Her brother William Charles was present at her death. She did not leave a Will. In her Administration dated 1898 it says "spinster without parent...to Eliza Chandler of No.1 Rosebery Terrace, West Ewell aforesaid Widow the natural and lawful sister and one of the next of kin, £41".

The Children and descendants of Thomas and Louisa Ditch[37]

Elizabeth Rosina's great-great-grandchild and Louisa Ditech's first child **Lucy Agnes Ditch** was born between 1784 and 1786. In 1894 she married Walter Tidmarsh, a boot maker, in St. Mary Newington. In 1901 when they lived with Lucy's parents in Lambeth they had two children **Lucy** born 1897 and **Louie** 1899 about whom nothing further is known. Walter Tidmarsh died in 1934.

Louisa Ditch's second child **Caroline Sarah Ditch** was born in 1880. In 1899 she married widower George Jones. He was a fruiterer. His first wife probably was Rosette Jones and they had two children: **George F. Jones** born 1889 and probably also **Rosa May** born in 1892. Nothing is known about the son called George. Rosa May, a shop assistant, lived with her father in 1911. Caroline Jones had four children: **Caroline Ethel Jones** born 1900, **Dorothy Blanche Jones** born 1901, **William Thomas Jones** born 1905 and **Albert Charles Jones** born 1906.

Louisa Ditch's third child **Thomas Ditch** was born in 1885. In 1891 he lived with his parents in Lambeth. He probably died in Wandsworth in 1951.

Louisa Ditch's fourth child **Charles Ditch** was born in 1885. In 1891 and 1901 he lived with his parents in Lambeth. He was a messenger at Lloyds Exchange. He probably married Ellen between 1902-1911.

Louisa Ditch's fifth child **Joseph John** [also known as Topher] **Ditch** was born in 1886. In 1891 and 1901 he lived with his parents in Lambeth.

---

[37] Information taken from Census 1841, 1851, 1861, 1871, 1881, 1891, 1901, 1911 and from Freebmd

He was a messenger at Lloyds Exchange. In 1911 he lived with his father. In 1913 he married Elizabeth Mary Champ.

Louisa Ditch's sixth child **Leonora Ditch** was born in 1888. In 1901 she lived with her parents. Nothing else is known about her.

Louisa Ditch's seventh child **Clara Ditch** was born in 1891. In 1901 she lived with her parents. In 1911 she was a servant in Brixton. Shortly afterwards she married widower Alfred John Gray born 1922. He was a waiter, later a lift attendant. They lived in Newington and had one son Alfred John Grey born 1912. Her husband was still alive at the time of her death in 1935. He died in 1961.

Louisa Ditch's eighth child **Elizabeth Ditch** was born in 1893. In 1901 she lived with her parents. Nothing else is known about her. She married George T. Vowles in Wandsworth in 1915 and had two daughters: Ivy F. Vowles born 1915 and Bessie L. Vowles born 1918.

The Children and descendants of Robert and Elizabeth Chandler[38]

Elizabeth Rosina's great grandchild and Eliza Chandler's first child, **Henry Chandler**, was born in 1873 at Guildford. In 1891 he lived in his parents' household and was a "general labourer". In 1901 he lived at Pinecroft, Crutchfield Road, Walton on Thames, with his wife Florence Jane, born in 1877, and a son Henry F. Chandler, born 1901. He was a "carpenter". By 1911 he lived at Sunbury Lane, Walton on Thames, with wife Florence Jane and three children: **Henry Frederick Chandler** born about 1901, **Florence Emma Chandler**, born about 1802, and **Frank Chandler** born about 1909.

Eliza Chandler's second child was **Louisa Jane Chandler** born in 1874. In 1881 she lived with her parents in Wonersh. In 1891 she was a servant in Guildford and then married George Harrington.

Eliza Chandler's third child, **William Alfred Chandler** was born in 1876 in Wonersh, Surrey. In 1891 he lived with his parents and was a "general labourer". He married Selina Ann Crane in 1899. In 1901 he was a "house painter" at Christchurch, Southwark. His son **Alfred H. Chandler** was born in 1901 and another son **William Alexander**

---

[38] Information taken from Census 1841, 1851, 1861, 1871, 1881, 1891, 1901, 1911 and from Freebmd

Chandler was born in 1902. They also had an adopted son Albert J. Crane Chandler, born in 1890 at Southwark. Selina Ann died about 1909 and William Alfred married a new wife Edith Mary. By 1911 he was a "house painter" at 17 Jervis Road, Fulham, with his wife and sons.

Eliza Chandler's fourth child, **Rose Chandler** was born in 1878 and her fifth child, **Lily Chandler** in 1878. They were twins. In 1881 they both lived with their parents. In 1891 Rose – at the age of 12! – was a servant in Bromley. In 1896 she gave birth to an illegitimate son Albert Chandler. In 1901 she was a servant in Barnes and her son lived with her parents in Walton. Lily Chandler died as a child.

Eliza Chandler's sixth child, **Annie Chandler** was born about 1880. She lived with her parents in 1891 and 1901. During the next decade she married Arthur Henry Watson who died in 1904. She died in 1909. they did not have any children.

Eliza Chandler's seventh child, **Ethel Chandler**, was born in 1883. She is listed with her parents in 1891. Nothing is known about her after that.

Eliza Chandler's eighth child **Eliza Chandler** was born in 1885. She lived with her parents in 1809. In 1911 she was a servant at Walton on Thames. She probably married Ivan Emery in Epsom in 1917.

Eliza Chandler's ninth child, **Minnie Chandler**, was born about 1886. She lived with her parents in 1891 and in 1901 she was a servant at Walton on Thames or Croydon.

Eliza Chandler's tenth child, **Robert Chandler** was born about 1891. In 1911 he lived with his widowed mother at Sunbury Lane in Walton on Thames.

George Anthony Kammel

George Anthony was born on 18 July 1775, baptized two months later on 2 September. At the time of Anthony Kammel's death he was 9 years old.

In 1778he became apprenticed with William Bennison as a japanner.[39]

---

[39] UK Register of Duties Paid for Apprentices' Indentures, 1710-1811

There is little information about him. It is possible that his surname was misspelled in marriage records, such as the one for a person called George Hammell in London at the time.[40]

There is a 1828 burial record of a George Kammel, aged 55 of St. Pancras, at Spa Field Burial Ground. Anthony Kammel's son would have been 53 at the time.

There is another George Kammel burial record dated 8 October 1784 at Norton St. Mary in Kent. It does not give the age of the deceased, but since he is described as a Gent he is unlikely to have been Anthony's son George who would have been nine years old at the time. Given that Anthony died shortly before the burial, it was most likely Anthony Kammel himself.[41]

Henry Christian John Kammel

Henry Christian John was born on 27 November 1777 and baptized on 21 December. At the time of Anthony Kammel's death he was 6 years old.[42]

In 1792 he became apprenticed with William Bennison as a japanner.[43] He could not read and write and was unable to sign his name when he married. His first marriage, to Patty Sophia Searle, took place in St. Giles parish at Cripplegate in 1799. The witnesses were Samuel Searle and [illeg] Barry.[44]

---

[40] Two marriages were recorded for George Hammell, one to Mary Ann Ilton in 1798 when he would have been 23 years old and one to Grace Richards eight years later. The children of the second marriage were Grace Ann Hammel born 1806 in Whitechapel, Sophia Hammell born 1814 in Southwark and Sarah Hammell born 1824 in Lambeth. The 1881 Census gives Rosina Hammel born 1831 in Southwark, who died in 1886.
George Hammell x Mary Ann Milton 26 February 1798 at St Martin in the Fields Westminster. [IGI]; George Hammell X Grace Richards 9 February 1806 at St. Giles Cripplegate. [IGI]; Grace Ann Hammel born 15 November 1806 ch. 25 January 1807 at St. Mary Whitechapel [IGI]; Sophia Hammel born? July 1814 ch. 28 July 1814 at St. George the Martyr Southwark [IGI]; Sarah Hammel ch. 28 October 1824 at St. Mary Lambeth [IGI]; Hammell Rosina 62 St. Saviour 1d 52 December 1886
[41] George Kammel buried 28 September 1828 at Spa Field Burial Ground. [Nat.Bur.Ind.]
[42] He was buried in St. Anne's, Soho, in 1821. www.familysearch.org
[43] UK Register of Duties Paid for Apprentices' Indentures, 1710-1811
[44] 5 December 1799 Henry Christian John Kammel married Patty Sophie Searle, St. Giles, Cripplegate; his mark – illiterate [LMA]

93

Their daughter Elizabeth Ann Camels [sic] baptized in 1800 at St. Giles, was presumably named after his sister and mother. In the birth register, the father's occupation is given as japanner.[45]

He – or someone with the same name - had a second daughter, also called Elizabeth Ann, but by a different wife called Martha, in 1811. The child was baptized at St. Anne's Soho. Burial records for Patty Sophia, the first wife, and the first Elizabeth Ann daughter have not been found. There is no record of his marriage to Martha.[46] He also had a son with Martha called George Antonio who was baptised at St. James in Westminster in 1806.[47]

The idea of Henry Christian John's second marriage is contradicted by the marriage of Robert Hayes and Sophia Kammel in 1829. If Sophia Kammel was still alive at the time of her marriage to Robert Hayes in 1829, Henry Christian John Kammel could not have been a widower who married Martha before 1811.

The entry in the Bishops Transcripts of marriages says that they were both widowed.[48] The original register does not exist, having been destroyed during the second world-war. Could there be a mistake in the transcript?

There is also confusion caused by Henry Christian John and Henry James sharing the same Christian name.

The Henry Cammel who married Frances Cox in 1797 at St. Ann's, Westminster, could not have been the illiterate Henry Christian John, because he signed his name. It could not have been Henry James either, as according to the marriage licence the groom was 21 years old. While Henry Christian John was over 20 at the time, his brother Henry James was only 17.

---

[45] 14 April 1800 Elizabeth Ann Camels, f.John m.Patty Sophia, St. Giles, Cripplegate [IGI]
[46] 16 June 1811 Elizabeth Ann Kammel, f.John Christian m.Martha, St. Ann West [IGI]
[47] www.familysearch.com
[48] Church of St. John the Evangelist, Smith's Square, Bishops Transcripts, Marriages: "Robert Hayes a Widower of this Parish and Sophia Kammel a Widow of this Parish were married in this church by Banns this Third Day of March in the year 1829 by me Henry Atcheson Offt. Minister, The marriage was solemnised between us Rober Hays S.K. x her mark In the presence of John Astell, J.H.Arrow No.425 [LMA]

In 1809 a John Camell married Ann Marr at St. George's Hanover Square. He did not sign the register, she did. Was it Henry Christian John's second marriage, making the one to Martha a third one?

There were a few other grooms called John Cammell, but none of them likely to have been Henry Christian John.[49]

Henry James Kammel

Henry James was born on 22 October 1780 and baptized three weeks later on 12 November. At the time of Anthony Kammel's death he was 3 years old.

When he grew up he became a currier. There is no record of his apprentiship.

In 1797 a Henry Cammel probably married Frances Cox at St. Ann, Westminster. He claimed to be 21 years old. He could sign his name, but had he been Anthony Kammel's son Henry James he would have been only 17.

Sometime before 1816 Henry Cammell could have married a second wife Rebecca.

There were two children, both called Henry, one baptized in 1816 at St. Lukes in Finsbury and the other at St. Giles in Cripplegate a year later. Their father was working as a porter and therefore was probably not Kammel's son Henry James.[50]

Sometime before 1818 Henry Cammell could have married a third wife, Elizabeth.

---

[49] In 1818 a John Cammell married Elizabeth Eliker in Marylebone He was a widower and signed the register, she was a spinster and entered only a mark. It was almost certainly not our John. In 1821 a John Cammall married Ann Randall at St. George Hanover Square. In 1822 a John Cummill married Sarah Matilda Tilley in St. Leonard Shoreditch. They had a son Robert Fulforth Cammell born in 1826 and baptized 1831. The father was very likely not Henry Christian John Kammel.

[50] 18 February 1816 Henry Cammell, f.Henry m.Rebecca, St. L Finsbury[IGI]; 25 May 1817 Henry Cammall, f.Henry m.Rebecca, St. Giles Cripplegate [IGI]

There were twin daughters, Mary Ann Cammell and Susana Cammell, baptized in 1818 at St. Martin-in-the-Fields.[51] Their address was Russell Place, 9 Bow Street. The father was a currier.

In 1822 James Cammell, a tallow chandler from Union Walk, and Martha Tilley had a child baptized also Martha at St. Luke's Shoreditch. No marriage certificate has been found. This James is unlikely to have been the same person as Henry James Kammel.[52]

The social standing of Kammel's descendants

Anthony Kammel's father was a forester on the estate of Count Vincent Waldstein. Before 1781 all people living on estates needed a permission from the estate owner for things like moving away, apprenticing their children to learn a trade or to study. Count Waldstein noticed Anthony Kammel was a bright child and became his patron, encouraging him in furthering his education and travelling abroad. For Kammel this meant a change in his social standing: a son of a serf he was able to join the young gentlemen who were studying, playing music and travelling. Formally, however, he still for the rest of his life continued with his responsibilities towards the Count to whom he wrote and sent his reports.

Kammel was not just a good musician, he had a charismatic personality and he was ambitious. He dreamt about being a court musician and marrying a rich and beautiful wife. He did not succeed in either of these dreams, but he managed to live his life on the edge of high society. Occasionally he played at Court concerts, he had friends not just among the German musicians in England, but also among the English nobility. He lived in a fashionable house in Mayfair. In spite of his constant financial struggle, he appeared to be rich.

Below this almost-upper-class appearance, however, there was ticking the mind of a prudent working man. In his last Will he wished his sons to be apprenticed, thus placing them safely in a middle class. For his daughter Elisabeth Rosina he left a dowry – large enough to attract a middle class man. He protected her from unsuitable marriage by attaching a condition that the dowry was payable only if the executors

---

[51] 23 July 1818 Mary Ann Cammell, f.Henry m.Elizabeth, St. Martin Westm, currier [IGI]; 23 July 1818 Susana Cammell. f.Henry m.Elizabeth, St. Martin Westm [IGI]
[52] 25 December 1822 Martha Cammell, f.James m.Martha, St. Luke Shoreditch [IGI]

agreed with the match. In the end she married a craftsman – a japanner. Japanning was a craft with a high social standing. Two of her brothers also became japanners.

The second generation slipped downwards on the social scale. Her second brother became a currier. It is interesting to note that, in spite of Kammel's plans for the social standing of his children, one of his sons was illiterate. Elisabeth Rosina, the oldest among the surviving children, could read and write. This could have been due to her position in the family or to her personality. After becoming a widow she married a clerk of the Duke of York, thus moving a step nearer to the world her father had dreamt of.

The second and further generations moved from Mayfair eastwards towards the City and beyond. Later some of them moved south across the river to Southwark and later still to the smaller places in Surrey. This geographic shift was accompanied with a slide down the social scale. Some of the third and fourth generation were no longer craftsmen, but labourers and servants in Surrey.

Of the white collar workers, there were two clerks, two messengers, one accountant and one solicitor. The accountant and solicitor were not successful. They both stopped working early in life – one died as an invalid and the other in a lunatic asylum.

Only two of the descendants – brother and sister - were teachers of music. They were both children of the eldest son of Kammel's eldest daughter. It would be interesting to know if it was her who tried to keep up the music tradition in the family.

The information we have about Kammel's later descendants is fragmentary, based mostly on the Census reports. A trend seems to emerge suggesting that from the fifth generation on the social class of Kammel's descendants was on the rise again.

Today, somewhere in the southern suburbs of London and in the towns and villages of Surrey, there may be people related to Anthony Kammel who do not know what a remarkable ancestor they once had. Possibly they travel to work on the Southern Railway to their white collar jobs in the City and in Westminster. All of them are descended from Anthony Kammel's daughter Elizabeth Rosina.

How Kammel is remembered in written sources

Eighteenth century

Leopold Mozart during his visit to London in 1765 noted Kammel's name in his diary. The name is listed next to that of the violoncellist Zappa. Leopold Mozart must have met them both at a social occasion. No further information is given in the diary.[1]

The family of James Harris were keen music lovers of the period. The family papers, published in 2001, contain a number of references to Kammel, giving details of concerts in which Kammel took part and of the cost of subscriptions. Apart from statements like "a very fine concert it was", their letters and diaries give the impression that attending a concert was first and foremost a social occasion.[2]

Another contemporary, John Marsh, himself a composer, gives information about Kammel's compositions which he liked to play with his friends. Kammel's own performance at a concert, however, disappointed him.[3]

A strong criticism of Kammel's ability as a violinist and a composer was expressed by an anonymous author calling himself ABC Diario Musico. Since he was very critical towards other musicians as well, his was perhaps not an unbiased opinion.[4]

A significant indicator of Kammel's social standing may be the fact that Mrs. Papendiek did not mention him by name in her journals although she wrote about many other musicians who used to play at Court.[5]

In the year of Kammel's death, a German music almanac by Forkel carried an article containing some mistakes: Kammel was not a German, nor did he play in the King's Band in London.[6]

A few years after Kammel's death a German guide for music lovers described the qualities of Kammel's music as follows:

---

[1] Mozart, Wolfgang Amadeus (1776) v.1. p.192
[2] Burrows, Donald & Dunhill, Rosemary (2001)
[3] Marsh, John (1998)
[4] *ABC Dario Musico* (1780)
[5] Papendiek, Charlotte Louisa Henrietta (1887).
[6] Forkel, Johann Nicolaus (1784) pp.89-90

"His feelings are often as tender as those of Pugnani and as delicate as those of Philidor and always as beautiful and true as those of Abel. He is aware of the nature and the limitations of his instruments and is able to use this knowledge to the best advantage of musical truth. Kammel understands how to blend colours and to contrast light and shade, his melodies are beautiful and his harmony excellent. His style is full, rounded and compact – and yet always transparent".[7]

Nineteenth century

At the beginning of the nineteenth century Kammel was mentioned in a French music dictionary by Choron, making some more mistakes: Kammel was not the King's flautist, nor did he die in Prague.[8]

The English music dictionary by Sainsbury had some new and accurate facts: that Kammel was born in Bohemia, studied with Tartini and was celebrated in Prague for his adagio playing. However, there were some mistakes: he was not a violinist in the King's Band, he did not marry a rich woman and he did not die in 1788.[9]

Apart from these two sources, Kammel was almost completely forgotten.

First half of the twentieth century

Baker's biographical dictionary of musicians in its first edition 1905 and later revised editions, such as the one published in 1940, does not have anything about Kammel.[10]

A Czech music dictionary by Pazdírek published before the second world-war gave as its source Dlabacz. It contained just one error:

---

[7] *Portefeuille fur Musikliebhaber* (1792). Translated by Norman Chapman:
"Fühlt oft so innigst wie Pugnani, oft so zärtlich wie Philidor, und immer wie Abel, schön, wahr. Er kennt die Natur und Genzen seiner Instrumente zum Vortheil der Wahrheit. Weiss Veflössung, und geschickte Austheilung des Lichts und Schadens, ist melodisch schön, und harmonisch vorstreflich; - und setzt voll, rund, compress – und doch durchsichtig".
[8] Choron, Alexandre Etien & Fayolle, Francois Joseph (1810) v.1 p.362
[9] Sainsbury (1824) v.2 p.3
[10] Baker, Theodore. *A biographical dictionary of musicians*. New York: Schirmer, 1900; *Baker's biographical dictionary of musicians*, 4th ed. Rev. & enl. New York: Schirmer, 1940

Kammel did no get to London in 1774. The date of Kammel's death was only given only as "before 1788".[11]

A mid-twentieth century book on orchestra by Carse pointed out that Kammel was one among the small number of viola players in his time.[12]

A 1945 Italian biography of Tartini by Capri mentioned the name of Kammel as one of Tartini's pupils. It gave a wrong date of Kammel's birth (he was born in 1740 not 1730) and only an approximate date of his death, "morto prima del 1788".[13]

Second half of the twentieth century

In the second half of the twentieth century Kammel was mentioned in quite a number of books and studies:

A history of Czech music by Racek unfortunately repeated the errors of its predecessors as to the date of his death and his working at Court.[14]

A carefully compiled German article by Cudworth in a music encyclopaedia contained some errors also, some of which the author was aware of: The author expressed the possibility that 1788 was not the date of Kammel's death but of his withdrawal from the music scene and it was not certain that he died in London, placing a question mark in brackets after the place name; Kammel was not a member of the Court Band (The author said it was alleged -"angeblich"); and he did not marry a rich wife. Charles Cudworth was the Curator of the Pendlebury Library of Music in Cambridge.[15]

A Czech book about Haydn's contemporaries by Poštolka repeated the usual errors about the date of his arrival to London and about being a royal musician.[16]

An English study of the classical sonata by Newman mentioned Kammel only briefly and pointed out the link between him and Bach and Abel.[17]

---

[11] Pazdírek, Oldřich (1937) p.522
[12] Carse, Adam von Ahn (1940) p.80
[13] Capri, Antonio (1945) p.388
[14] Racek, Jan (1958) p.177
[15] Cudworth, Charles L. (1958) v.7 col.466-7
[16] Poštolka, Milan (1961) pp.106-108
[17] Newmann, William S. (1963) p.736

Similarly, the monograph about Bach by Terry spoke about the help Bach gave to Kammel in London. The text repeated the mistake about the date of Kammel's arrival in London, citing Rieman as a source.[18]

The history of the violin by Van der Straeten devoted a page to Kammel, repeating some of the usual mistakes and giving the date of Kammel's death as 1788. He quoted Pohl and Dlabacz as his sources.[19]

A German monograph about Abel by Knape contained a brief reference to Kammel, again giving the wrong date for his arrival in London.[20]

In a paper to a Haydn conference, Zdeňka Pilková compared the work of Kammel and Haydn. There were a few errors: Kammel did not come to London in 1764, but a year later.[21] She wrote an article about Kammel for the 1980 edition of The New Grove and two papers about Kammel's compositions - *Sonata in A for Violin and Basso Continuo, Sinfonia in G* and *Sinfonia in D*.[22]

In his thesis on eighteenth century concert life in Bath, James gave a brief and accurate account of Kammel.[23]

In the second half of the 1980s Eva Mikanová drew attention to the correspondence of Kammel with Count Waldstein. All the details in her brief paragraph about Kammel are accurate. She is the only author to point out that Kammel was actually a "podanný" (serf) of Count Waldstein. That explains why Kammel in his letters to Waldstein was asking for permission to extend his stay in London.[24]

Mikanová's second article gave more details about Kammel's life in Britain, mentioning a biography of Kammel, by one of his relations written in 1911 and presumably unpublished. It apparently contains a story about a threat of violence which made him leave Vienna. The threat was not connected with a woman, but with jealousy concerning his musical success. Another unconfirmed story in this biography tells about the Queen of England overhearing his solo violin playing in church and

---

[18] Terry, Charles Sanford (1967) p.115
[19] Straeten, Edmund Sebastien Joseph van der (1968) v.1 p.219
[20] Knape, Walter (1973) p.68
[21] Pilková, Zdeňka (1981)
[22] Pilková, Zdeňka (1980); Pilková, Zdeňka & Gerlach, Sonja (1982); Pilková, Zdeňka (1984)
[23] James, Kenneth Edward (1987) p.737
[24] Mikanová, Eva (1988) p.183

inviting him to Court. In one of his letters Kammel actually said that Bach had told the Queen about him.[25] According to this biography Kammel died in London and was buried there. Neither of these facts are certain. The biography goes on to say that his Cremona violin was still in the Kammel family in the 1870s, but its present whereabouts were not known. Mikanová thinks this source to be unreliable. The rest of her article gives a summary of some of the main facts from Kammel's correspondence which are highly informative.[26]

McVeigh in his book about eighteen century violinists summarised facts about Kammell on two pages. He avoided repeating the errors of earlier authors, except for saying that "Kammell is reputed to have entered into a rich marriage, perhaps in 1782, after which he is not known as a concert performer".[27]

Graham Melville-Mason in his paper on musicians of Bohemia gave a brief paragraph on Kammel.[28]

A Czech article about the Will of Kammel by Zdeňka Pilková and Sylva Šimsová contains minor errors: He did not arrive in 1764 but in the spring of 1765. He had 8 children, not 7. The date of his death – 5 October 1784 – has since become known.[29] Subsequent discussion was published in the same periodical a year later.[30]

A Czech 1989 conference paper by Michaela Freemanová about Kammel in London was published in 1994. The author said that Kammel's last public appearance was his benefit concert in May 1781. Advertisements show that two more concerts were announced: one in Salisbury in March 1782 and a benefit concert in London in May 1782. There is no published evidence that the two concerts would have been cancelled. Newbury was not a horse racing centre as the author said. In Kammel's time it was a small market town. Horse racing was introduced in 1805, long after Kammel's death. The author expressed her doubt about Kammel's death and mentioned the possibility that he may have died on the Continent.[31]

---

[25] Freemanová, Michaela & Mikanová, Eva (2003b) p.214
[26] Mikanová, Eva (1989)
[27] McVeigh, Simon (1989) pp.85-6
[28] Melville-Mason, Graham (1989) p.102
[29] Pilková, Zdeňka & Šimsová, Sylva (1993)
[30] Freemanová, Michaela, Pilková, Zdeňka, Šimsová, Sylva, & Kuna, Milan (1994)
[31] Freemanová, Michaela (1994)

An article about Kammel's Will by Zdeňka Pilková and Sylva Šimsová summarised facts found in London with some minor errors: He came to London in 1765 not 1764. He is named in Leopold Mozart travel notes for 1764 to 1765, not 1764. In addition to the seven children mentioned in the article, another child, Lucy born in 1769, has since been discovered. Kammel's daughter, Elizabeth Rosina, was not the Elisabeth Cammell buried at Bunhill Street. The footnote on p.94 also contained an error: Lady Lucy Mann, a dedicatee of one of Kammel's compositions, was not the wife of the British representative in Florence, but of his identically named nephew. The nephew married Lucy Noel in 1765 and they had a daughter called Lucy christened 2 April 1766 in St. James, Westminster.[32]

A study of eighteenth century concerts outside London by Burchell mentioned Kammel in passing. Tables contained statistical information about the repertoire used in the concerts.[33]

In 1988 the reminiscences of Kammel's contemporary John Marsh were made available.[34]

Michaela Freemanová published an article about Kammel's correspondence in 1999. It described Kammel's unsuccessful commercial activities on behalf of Count Waldstein. It also revealed a few details of Kammel's personal life, for instance his journey North in 1766 when he sent a letter to the Count from "Edenbourg in Ireland".[35]

Information about Freemasonry can be found in an article by McVeigh, mentioning Kammel's name.[36]

Family papers of Kammel's contemporary James Harris were published in 2001.[37]

In 2001 a new edition of Baker's biographical dictionary of musicians was published, edited by Nicholas Slonimsky.[38] It contains brief information about Kammel which is more or less accurate, except for the usual errors

[32] Pilková, Zdeňka & Šimsová, Sylva (1995)
[33] Burchell, Jenny (1996)
[34] Marsh, John (1998)
[35] Freemanová, Michaela (1999)
[36] McVeigh, Simon (2000)
[37] Burrows, Donald & Dunhill, Rosemary (2001)
[38] Baker, Theodore (2001)

about the time and place of his death and about him having been a court musician.

The New Grove *Dictionary of Music and Musicians* has an article about Kammel by Zdeňka Pilková which is informative and mostly correct, with the exception of the number of Kammel's children.[39]

In the same year, drawing on Kammel's correspondence, Freemanová described Kammel's incognito travels through Britain with "A Certain Mr. Nouelle".

One of Kammel's supporters called Lord "Thenham"[40] has not been identified in her paper. The place name Tenham appears in a variety of spellings, among others Teynham and Thenham. The person in the correspondence was most likely Henry Roper 11th Baron of Teynham (1733-1793). He was a Catholic. His main seat was Lynsted in Kent.

Later on in her paper Freemanová mentions an Esq. Tay[lor]. It appears that "Esq. Taylor" was an unidentified supporter of Kammel, described by him as a Baron and rich landowner, possibly the same person as "Lord Thenham".[41]

A German article in a new edition of a music encyclopaedia by Freemanová contains a well informed and accurate article about Kammel. It includes information from Kammel's correspondence with Count Waldstein.[42]

Another article by Freemanová from the same year summarises the main points from Kammel's correspondence with Count Waldstein. It confirms that Kammel was a Roman Catholic. In a footnote it summarises the origin of the mistaken notion about Kammel being a court musician. Lord Thenham and Esq. Solis are described by Kammel in his letter as "who is a Baron to whom I give lessons". It is not clear from the article to whom of these two the description applies to – logically it should be Thenham because Sole (not Solis) was not a Baron. The author mentions also a Mr. Taylor with whom Kammel was staying at one time. As mentioned above, this could have been Lord Thenham. In a footnote 17 on p.228 she mentions that the name Henry Taylor appears on a

---

[39] Pilková, Zdeňka (2001)
[40] Freemanová, Michaela (2001) p.17; fn.5 on p.21
[41] Freemanova Michaela (2001) p.18; fn.9 on p.21
[42] Freemanová, Michaela (2003a) Personenteil 9, col.1432-3

music manuscript of a part of Kammel's violin sonata in the British Library under shelfmark R.M.21.d.16. I have checked this manuscript in the British Library and have not seen; any such name on it. It must be a mistake in the citation.[43]

McVeigh in his contribution to a 2005 book about concert life in 18th century Britain calls Kammel a "less significant composer" and a violinist "whose quartets were sporadically performed".[44]

[43] Freemanová, Michaela & Mikanová, Eva (2003b)
[44] Wollenberg, Susan & McVeigh, Simon (2004) p.175; p.179

APPENDICIES

APPENDIX I

Chronology of Kammel's documented concerts in Britain

Abbreviations
Bath Chr = *Bath Chronicle*
GZ = *Gazetter*
PA = *Public Advertiser*
McV db = *Calendar of London concerts 1750-1800* (Simon McVeigh)
MH = *Morning Herald*
SJ = *Salisbury Journal*
SWJ = *Salisbury and Winchester Journal*
ZPnts = manuscript notes of Zdeňka Pilková

1766, February   first concert
LONDON
Freemanová, Michaela (2003b) p.216;

1767, January 27
STAMFORD
Freemanová, Michaela (2003b) p.216;

1768, May 6   K benefit
LONDON   KING STREET, ALMACK'S ROOMS
PA 1/3, 2/3, 12/3, 21/4, 22/4, 27/4, 28/4, 3/5, 4/5, 5/5, 6/5
McV db; ZPnts; Freemanová, Michaela (2003b) p.217;

1768, November 9
BATH
James, Kenneth Edward (1987) p.737; Freemanová, Michaela (2003b) p.220;

1768, November 17
BATH
James, Kenneth Edward (1987) p.737; Freemanová, Michaela (2003b) p.220;

1769, February 6   K lead
LONDON   ST JAMES'S STREET, THACHED HOUSE TAVERN
PA 27/1
McV db; ZPnts;

1769, March 9   K lead
LONDON   BREWER STREET, HICKFORD'S ROOMS
PA 9/2
McV db; ZPnts;

1769, April 20   K benefit
LONDON   KING STREET, ALMACK'S ROOMS
PA 8/4, 13/4
McV db; ZPnts;

1769, April 27   K lead
LONDON   BREWER STREET, HICKFORD'S ROOMS
PA 13/4
McV db; ZPnts;

1769, December 14
BATH   GYDE'S ROOM
Bath Chr. 14/12/1769
Cowgill, Rachel & Holman, Peter (2007) p.144;

1770, March 5
WINCHESTER
SJ 3/9

1770, March 22
LONDON   BREWER STREET, HICKFORD'S ROOMS
GZ 22/3; PA 6/3
McV db; ZPnts;

1770, April 10
LONDON   THROCKMORTON
Burrows, Donald & Dunhill, Rosemary (2001) p.587;

1770, May 17   K benefit
LONDON   KING STREET, ALMACK'S ROOMS
PA 1/5, 5/5, 7/5, 10/5, 14/5, 15/5, 16/5, 17/5
McV db; ZPnts;

1771, March 11
LONDON   BREWER STREET, HICKFORD'S ROOMS
PA news
McV db; ZPnts;

1771, May 9   K benefit
LONDON   BREWER STREET, HICKFORD'S ROOMS
PA 9/5
McV db; ZPnts;

1771, October 25   K lead
SALISBURY
SJ 21/10
Burrows, Donald & Dunhill, Rosemary (2001) p.651;

1772, March 23
LONDON   ANSON
Burrows, Donald & Dunhill, Rosemary (2001) p.666;

1772, April 25
SHUGBOROUGH
www.imagining;

1772, May 7   K benefit
LONDON   BREWER STREET, HICKFORD'S ROOMS
PA 6/5, 7/5
McV db; ZPnts;

1772, September 30 K lead
SALISBURY
SWJ 14/9, 21/9, 28/9
Burrows, Donald & Dunhill, Rosemary (2001) p.684;

1773, May 7   K benefit
LONDON   BREWER STREET, HICKFORD'S ROOMS
PA 31/3, 6/5, 7/5
McV db; ZPnts;

1773, July 14
BLANDFORD   GREAT ASSEMBLY ROOM, BLANDFORD FORUM
Freemanová, Michaela (2003b); Burrows, Donald & Dunhill, Rosemary
(2001) p.735;

1774, January 28
LONDON
Burrows, Donald & Dunhill, Rosemary (2001) p.759;

1774, April 29   K benefit
LONDON   BREWER STREET, HICKFORD'S ROOMS
PA 15/4, 22/4, 23/4, 26/4, 27/4, 28/4, 29/4
McV db; ZPnts;

1774, July 19
BLANDFORD
Burrows, Donald & Dunhill, Rosemary (2001) p.768;

1774, August 14
SALISBURY
SWJ 22/8

1774, September 24
SALISBURY
SJ 22/8
Burrows, Donald & Dunhill, Rosemary (2001) p.771;

1775, April 3
LONDON   BREWER STREET, HICKFORD'S ROOMS
PA 8/3, 11/3, 13/3, 15/3, 17/3. 21/3. 23/3, 28/3
McV db;

1775, April 28   K lead
LONDON   HANOVER SQUARE, HANOVER SQUARE ROOMS
PA 8/3, 15/3, 18/3, 21/3, 23/3, 25/3, 27/3, 28/3, 20/4, 21/4, 22/4, 24/4,
25/4,
McV db; ZPnts;

1775, May 5   K benefit
LONDON   BREWER STREET, HICKFORD'S ROOMS
PA 13/3, 7/4, 10/4, 21/4, 28/4, 2/5, 3/5, 4/5
McV db; ZPnts; Burrows, Donald & Dunhill, Rosemary (2001) p.826;

1775, October 4   K lead
SALISBURY
SWJ 31/7, 7/8, 14/8, 11/9,2/10
Burrows, Donald & Dunhill, Rosemary (2001) p.851;

1776, May 15   K benefit
LONDON   HANOVER SQUARE, HANOVER SQUARE ROOMS
PA 11/4, 25/4, 27/4, 29/4, 2/5, 6/5, 9/5, 10/5, 11/5, 13/5, 14/5
McV db; ZPnts; Burrows, Donald & Dunhill, Rosemary (2001) p.893;

1776, August 28
SALISBURY
SJ 26/8
Burrows, Donald & Dunhill, Rosemary (2001) p.907; Marsh, John (1998)

1777, May 9   K benefit
LONDON   HANOVER SQUARE, HANOVER SQUARE ROOMS
PA 7/4, 9/4, 24/4, 26/4, 1/5, 3/5, 5/5, 6/5, 7/5, 8/5, 9/5
McV db; ZPnts;

1777, June 5
LONDON   HANOVER SQUARE, HANOVER SQUARE ROOMS
PA 13/5, 14/5, 20/5, 21/5, 22/5, 23/5, 31/5, 2/6, 3/6, 4/6, 5/6
McV db; ZPnts; Burrows, Donald & Dunhill, Rosemary (2001) p.936;

1778, April 24
LONDON   TOTTENHAM STREET, TOTTENHAM STREET ROOMS
PA 22/4, 23/4, 24/4
McV db; ZPnts; Burrows, Donald & Dunhill, Rosemary (2001) p.979;

1778, May 8   K benefit
LONDON   TOTTENHAM STREET, TOTTENHAM STREET ROOMS
PA 28/3, 4/4, 6/4, 22/4, 24/4, 27/4, 29/4, 1/5, 4/5, 5/5, 6/5, 7/5, 8/5
McV db; ZPnts;

1778, September 9   K lead
WINCHESTER
Freemanová, Michaela (2003b) p.224;

1779, January 30
LONDON
Burrows, Donald & Dunhill, Rosemary (2001) p.1006;

1779, April 20
LONDON   TOTTENHAM STREET, TOTTENHAM STREET ROOMS
PA 10/4, 12/4, 19/4, 20/4
McV db; ZPnts;

1779, May 6   K benefit
LONDON   TOTTENHAM STREET, TOTTENHAM STREET ROOM
PA 10/4, 19/4, 3/5, 4/5, 5/5
McV db; ZPnts; Burrows, Donald & Dunhill, Rosemary (2001) p.1028

1779, May 24
LONDON   TOTTENHAM STREET, TOTTENHAM STREET ROOMS
PA 27/3 news?, 21/4, 26/4, 28/4, 1/5, 8/5, 17/5,19/5, 21/5, 24/5 news
McV db; ZPnts;

1780, May 19   K benefit
LONDON   TOTTENHAM STREET, TOTTENHAM STREET ROOMS
PA 25/4, 28/4, 17/5, 18/5, 19/5
McV db; ZPnts;

1781/, May 11   K benefit
LONDON   TOTTENHAM STREET, TOTTENHAM STREET ROOMS
PA 11/5
McV db; ZPnts;

1782, March 12
SALISBURY
SJ 4/3
Freemanová, Michaela (2003b) p.220

1782, May 10   K benefit
LONDON   SOHO SQUARE, CARLISLE HOUSE
MH 4/5, 6/5, 7/5, 8/5, 9/5, 10/5,
McV db; ZPnts;

YEAR	London	Bath	Blandford	Salisbury	Shugborough	Stamford	Winchester	TOTAL
1766	1							1
1767						1		1
1768	1	2						3
1769	4	1						5
1770	3			1				4
1771	2			1				3
1772	2			2				4
1773	1		1					2
1774	2		1	1	1			5
1775	3			1				4
1776	1			1				2
1777	2							2
1778	2						1	3
1779	4							4
1780	1							1
1781	1							1
1782	1						1	2
TOTAL	31	3	2	7	1	1	2	47

Kammel's Concerts by Place & Date

115

APPENDIX III

Publishers, vendors, printers and engravers

SELF/ London/ address unspecified

Sei Trii, di Violino e Basso, Op.1, 1766, [in BUCEM, in Moffat, in BL g.242.(12.)]
Early self-publication of first work:

SELF/ London/ 34 Half Moon Street, Piccadilly

Concurrently with the publication/republication of his early works by P. Welcker, Kammel himself published first editions of two new works. Both were later reissued by Welcker.

Six Duets for Two Violins, Op.5, 1768, [in BUCEM, in Moffat, in BL g.276.d]

Six Notturnos for Two Violins and a Bass, Op.6, 1772, [in BUCEM, in BL h.2782.gg.(3.)]
P. Welcker listed as joint vendor

Six Duettos for Two Violins, Op.11, 1780, [in BL g.218.ff.(4.)]

Six Divertimentos, Three for Two Violins, a Tenor and Violoncello, and Three for a Hautboy or German Flute, Two Violins and Violoncello, Op.14, 1780, [in BL g.276.b]

Six Duettos for Two Violins, Op.18, 1782, [in BL g.276.f]
Actually appeared under the imprint of Kerpen's Music Shop, but according to Moffat there is no record of any other publications by Kerpen, nor is he listed, in Kidson. Moffat is of the opinion that this was actually self-published by Kammel, with Kerpen acting as vendor. The argument seems plausible

Six Notturnos for Two Violins and Violoncello, Op.19, 1784, [in BUCEM, in BL g.276]

J. BETZ/ London/ 21 Rupert Street

Music seller, publisher and importer of foreign music c.1775-80 [Humphries p.70, not in Kidson]

Six Sonatas for the Pianoforte, Harpsichord or Harp with Accompaniments for a Violin and Violoncello, Op.9, 1780, [in BL h.1909.d]

Reissue, originally published by J. Welcker, but dated 1780, some years after J. Welcker's last previous publication of Kammel, so perhaps Welcker had by then lost interest/ given up publishing rights on Kammel's works. Certainly, Kammel's main publisher for his new works at that stage was John Preston, and not Welcker any more. N.B. Although issued, in London with French title pages, which is puzzling and suggests we may be dealing with some sort of a variant edition (either for export or for the French expatriate community).

BRODERIP & LONGMAN/ London/ 13 Haymarket & The Harp & Crown, 26 Cheapside

In 1780, they published reissues of Kammel's Op.3 and Op.6

CAULFIELD/ London/ 5 Piccadilly

Noted family of music engravers, known to have worked for P. Welcker, in the 1770s. John Caulfield the Elder was an engraver/printer at 5 Piccadilly c.1780-90. John Caulfield the Younger was at 36 Piccadilly c.1799 or earlier. [Kidson p.25]

Six Divertimentos, Three for Two Violins, a Tenor and Violoncello, and Three for a Hautboy or German Flute, Two Violins and a Violoncello, Op.14, 1780, [in BUCEM]

DE LA CHAVARDIERE/ Paris

Six Duets pour Deux Violins, Op.2, 1770, [in BL g.218.ff.(3.)]

Quatuors, Op.4, [ ], [in De la Chevardier catalogue 1779]

Trio Violons, [ ], 1774, [in De la Chevardier catalogue 1774]

Sonates à Violon seul, Op.10, 1772, [in De la Chevardier catalogue 1772]

Concerto Violons, Op.11, [ ], [in De la Chevardier catalogue 1772]

Concerto Violons, Op.12, [ ], [in De la Chevardier catalogue 1772]

Concerto Violons, Op.13, [ ], [in De la Chevardier catalogue 1772]

Trio Violons, Op.17, [ ], [in De la Chevardier catalogue 1777]

DURIEU/ Paris

Six Duo Concertants pour Deux Violons, Op.24, 1785, [in BL g.218.i.(8.)]

JOHN FENTUM'S MUSIC SHOP/ London/ 78 Strand, corner of Salisbury Street

Major retailer, engraver and later sometimes publisher also. [Kidson pp.25-26]
Did not publish any of Kammel's works, but the BL copies of Op.1 1780 reissue and Op.6 1780 reissue were purchased from Fentum's shop (both bear the company sticker).

M. GOTZ/ Mannheim

Six Sonates a Deux Violons, Op.2, 1779, [in BUCEM]

HUBERTY/ Paris

Six Quautors [sic] Concertante à Deux Violons, Alto et Violoncelle; Op.4, 1770 [in Huberty catalogue 1770]

B. HUMMEL/ Haag

Trio à Deux Violons, Flute trav. & Basse, Op.1, 1768, [in Hummel catalogue 1768]

Six Sonates à Deux Violons & Base, Op.1, 1775, [in BUCEM, in BL h.1909.a]

Six Sonates à Deux Violons, Op.2, 1767, [in Moffat]

Duo à Violons, Op.2, 1768, [in Hummel catalogue 1769]

Duos pour les Violins, Op.2, 1768, [in Hummel catalogue 1771]

Six Sonates à Deux Violons, Op.2, 1775, [in BUCEM, in BL g.411.(3.)]

Six Sonates 2vl & b, Op.3, 1770, [in Hummel catalogue 1770]

Trios à 2Violons & Basse, Op.3, 1770, [in Hummel catalogue 1771]

Ouverture, Op.4, 1770, [in Hummel catalogue 1770]

Six Quatuor, Op.4, 1771, [in Hummel catalogue 1771]

Six Sonatines 2vl & b, Op.6, 1772, [in Hummel catalogue 1772]

Trios à 2 Violons et Basse, Op.6, 1772, [in Hummel catalogue 1773]

Six Sonates à Deux Violons et Basse, Op.7, 1770, [in BUCEM, in BL g.276.c]

Six Sonates à Deux Violons et Basse, Op.7, 1775, [in BUCEM]

Six Sonates Pour le Violon Avec la Basse Continue, Op.9, 1765, [in Moffat]

Six Sonates Pour le Violon Avec la Basse Continue, Op.9, 1775, [in BUCEM, in BL g.276.e]

Solos à Violon et Basse, Op.9, 1776, [in Hummel catalogue 1776]

J. J. HUMMEL/ Amsterdam and Berlin

Six Quatuor 2vl, vla & vcl, Op.8, 1774, [in Hummel catalogue 1774]

Six Sonates cemb, vl, vcl, Op.10, 1776, [in Hummel catalogue 1776]

Trios pour le Clavecin, Op.10, 1776, [in Hummel catalogue 1776]

Ouverture, Op.11, 1776, [in Hummel catalogue 1776]

Six Simphonies, Op.11, 1777, [in Hummel catalogue 1781]

Duos pour Deux Violons, Op.12, 1778, [in Hummel catalogue 1781]

Quartets, Op.14, 1781, [in Hummel catalogue 1783]

Six Duos, Op.15, 1781, [in Hummel catalogue 1781]

Duos pour le Violon, Op.15, 1781, [in Hummel catalogue 1783]

Trios à Deux Violons et Basse, Op.16, 1781, [in Hummel catalogue 1783]

Six Trios à Deux Violons et Basse, Op.16, 1790, [in BUCEM, in BL g.420.c.(12.)]

Six Quatuors 3 for 2vl, vla, vcl; 3 for fl/ob 2vl vcl, Op.17, 1781, [in Hummel catalogue 1781]

Trios à 2 Violons & Basse - Bach, Abel, Kammel, [no Op.],1778, [in Hummel catalogue 1778]

KERPEN'S MUSIC SHOP/ London/ 19 Wardour Street, Soho Square

According to Humphries Kerpen was a publisher c 1782-85.
[not, in Kidson].

Listed as the publisher of Op.18 dated 1782, but Moffat is of the opinion that Kerpen was actually only the retailer, and that the publisher was more likely Kammel himself.

Six duettos for two violins, Op.18, 1776, [in Moffat]

Six duettos for two violins, Op.18, 1782, [in BUCEM]

LE MENU ET BOYER/ Paris

Pieces de clavecin arr. by Ch.Roeser, [no Op.], 1770 [in Le Menu et Boyer catalogue 1775

Trio, Op.3, 1772, [in Le Menu et Boyer catalogue 1772]

LONGMAN & BRODERIP/ London/ Harp and Crown, 26 Cheapside

Another large established firm of music sellers, publishers and printers which took over publication of some of Kammell's earlier works after Welcker's death.

In 1770 advertised as "musical instrument makers". Between 1771-1778 Longman, Lukey & Co, 1778-1779 Longman, Lukey & Broderip, and from 1780 until bankruptcy, in 1798 Longman & Broderip. [Kidson pp.72-74].

Duet for Two Violins, Op.2, 1778, [in Longman & B. catalogue 1778]

Duet for Two Violins, Op.2, 1781, [in Longman & B catalogue 1781]

Duet for Two Violins, Op.2, 1789, [in Longman & B catalogue 1789]

Trios, Op.3, 1778, [in Longman & B. catalogue 1778]

A Second Sett of Six Sonatas for Two Violins and a Bass, Op.3, 1780, [in BUCEM, in BL g.420.e.(5)]

Trios, Op.3, 1781, [in Longman & B. catalogue 1781]

Trio, Op.3, 1789, [in Longman & B. catalogue 1789]

Quartets, Op.4, 1778, [in Longman & B. catalogue 1778]

Quartet, Op.4, 1781, [in Longman & B. catalogue 1778]

Quartets, Op.4, 1789, [in Longman & B. catalogue 1789]

Notturno, Op.6, 1778, [in Longman & B. catalogue 1778]

Six Notturnos for Two Violins and a Bass, Op.6, 1780, [in BUCEM, in BL g.420.e.(4.)]

Notturno, Op.6, 1781, [in Longman & B. catalogue 1781]

Notturno, Op.6, 1789, [in Longman & B. catalogue 1789]

Trios, Op.7, 1778, [in Longman & B. catalogue 1778]

Violin Solos, Op.8, 1781, [in Longman & B. catalogue 1781]

Six Sonatas for the Pianoforte, Harpsichord or Harp with Accompaniments for a Violin and Violoncello, Op.9, 1781, [in Longman & B. catalogue 1781]

Six Sonatas for the Pianoforte, Harpsichord or Harp with Accompaniments for a Violin and Violoncello, Op.9, 1789, [in Longman & B. catalogue 1789]

Overtures Select, Op.10, 1781, [in Longman & B. catalogue1781]

Quartets, Op.12, 1778, [in Longman & B. catalogue 1778]

Quartets, Op.12, 1789, [in Longman & B. catalogue 1789]

S. MARKOLDT/ Amsterdam

Six Notturnos a Deux Violons et Basse, Op.6, 1770, [in Moffat, in BL g.218.u.(1.)]

Six Notturnos a Deux Violons et Basse, Op.6, 1780, [in BUCEM]

MASSINGHI'S ITALIAN WAREHOUSE/ London/ Dover Street, **Piccadilly.**

Listed as the retail outlet on Kammel's self-published edition of *Six Duets for Two Violins*, Op.5, 1770]

JOHN PRESTON/ London/ 97 Strand, near Beaufort Buildings

Main publisher for Kammel's new works from about 1778 to 1781. First recorded, in 9 Banbury Court off Long Acre circa 1774, moved to 105 Strand, in 1776, and 97 Strand, in 1778. Moffat's argument about the date of Kammel's first work for Preston centres on this move from 105 to 97 Strand. The entire company was eventually purchased by Novello. [Kidson p.106].

Six Notturnos for Two Violins and a Bass, Op.6, 1790, [in BUCEM]

Six Solos for the Violin with a Thorough Bass for the Harpsichord, Op.8, 1785, [in BUCEM]

Six Divertimentos for the Harpsichord or Piano-Forte, [no Op.], 1776 [in Moffat]

Six Duetts, Four for Two Violins, and Two for a Violin and Tenor, Op.15, 1780, [in BL g.218.(3.)]

Six Duetts, Four for Two Violins, and Two for a Violin and Tenor, Op.15, 1785, [in BUCEM]

Six Trios for Two Violins and a Violoncello with a Thorough Bass for the Harpsichord, Op.16, 1780, [in BL g.411.(6.)]

Six Trios for Two Violins and a Violoncello, with a Thorough Bass for Harpsichord, Op.16, 1785, [in BUCEM, in BL g.222.(12.)]

Six Divertimentos for a Violin and Tenor or Two Violins, Op.17, 1781, [in BUCEM, in BL h.219.a.(4.)]

Six Divertimentos for the Harpsichord or Piano-forte, Op.17, 1783, [in BUCEM, in BL g.276.g]

J. SCHMIDT/ Amsterdam

Six Quatuors a Deux Violons, Taille et Basse, Op.7, 1780, [in BUCEM, in BL g.276.a.(2.)]

Six Divertimentos pour Deux Violons ou Violon et Alto Viola, Op.17, 1790, [in BUCEM]

SIEBER/ Paris

Duo, Op.7, [ ], [in Sieber catalogue 1772]

Trio, Op.8, [ ], [in Sieber catalogue 1772]

Sonates, Op.13, [ ], [in Sieber catalogue 1774]

Six Quatuors pour Deux Violons Alto et Basse, OP.14, 1770, [in BUCEM, in BL h.1909.c]

Quatuours, Op.14, [ ], [in Sieber catalogue 1774]

Symphonies, Op.17, [ ], [in Sieber catalogue 1776]

Six Divertisement a Deux Violons, Alto et Violoncelle, Op.21, [ ], [in Sieber catalogue 1778]

Trios, Op.23, [ ], [in Sieber catalogue 1782]

Trios, Op.25, [ ], [in Sieber catalogue 1786]

T. STRAIGHT/ London/ St. Martin's Lane

Engraver

Six Notturnos for Two Violins and a Bass, Op.6, 1780, Longman & Broderip London [in BUCEM, in BL g.420.e.(4.)]

Six duettos for Two Violins, Op.18, 1782, Kerpen London [in BUCEM]

S. A. & P. THOMPSON/ 75 St. Paul's Churchyard

Large and long-established family of musical instrument makers, music printers, sellers and publishers. Exact initials that precede the name 'Thompson' vary from imprint to imprint. "S." stands for Samuel, "A." for Anne, "P." for Peter. Took over publication of some of Kammel's early works after Welcker's death, reusing old plates (merely substituting new name). [Kidson pp.125-30].

Sei Trii, di Violino e Basso, Op.1, 1780, [in BUCEM, g.420.e.(3)]

Six Duets for Two Violins, Op.2, 1778, [in BL g.218.z.(4.)]

Six Overtures, in Eight Parts by the following composers, I. Stamitz, II. Vanhall, III. Mislevecheck, IV. Princess Royal of Saxony, V. Hayden, VI. Vanhall, the whole collected by Antonio Kammel (arrangement), [no Op.], 1790, [in BUCEM]

VENIER/ Paris

Duetti per Due Violini, Op.3, 1773, [in Venier catalogue 1773]

Trio, Op.6, 1771, [in Venier catalogue 1771]

Trio per due violini & basso li qualli si potranno esequire e piena orchestra, Op.6, 1773, [in Venier catalogue 1773]

G. WALKER/ London/ 106 Gt. Portland Street

Six Divertimentos, as Quartets, Three for Two Violins, a Tenor and Violoncello, and Three for a German Flute or Hautboy, Two Violins and Violoncello, Op.12, 1800, [in BUCEM]

JOHN WELCKER/ 9 Haymarket, facing the Opera House

Son of P. Welcker. First recorded as a business, in 1776, but could have been operating earlier (in fact probably was, if he is already on record, in 1776). Address changed to 10 Haymarket, in 1778 which suggests a cut-off dates for Kammel publications between 1775 and early 1778, in 1780 moved to 18 Coventry Street, leaving the Haymarket business to his brother-in-law James Blundell. Kitson says: "His other publications consist, in a great measure of instrumental music by foreign composers, including Kammell" [Kidson pp.150-51]

Six Sonatas for the Pianoforte, Harpsichord or Harp with Accompaniments for a Violin and Violoncello, Op.9, 1775, [in BUCEM h.2999.(2.)]

Six Notturnos for Two Violins and Violoncello, Op.19, 1785, [in BUCEM]

Six Dancing Minuets, in Three Parts for Two Violins and a Bass, 1775, [in BUCEM]

Six Sonatas for Two Violins and a Violoncello, composed by Messrs. Bach, Abel and Kammell (compilation), [no Op.], 1777, [in BL g.420.e.(6.), in BL g.425.(1.), in BL R.M.17.c.3.(14.), in BL g.415.(1.)]

PETER WELCKER/ 17 Gerrard Street, St. Ann's, Soho

Kammel's main publisher from about 1769/1770 to 1775/1776. Died 1775. Business continued at the same address by his widow, probably under the management of James Blundell who had married into the family, until her death, in 1778. After this date Kammel's works were being reissued by other publishers. [Kidson pp.150-51].

Sei Trii, di Violino e Basso, Op.1, 1770, [in BL g.415.(4.); in BL R.M.17.c.6.(9)]

Six Duetts for Two Violins, Op.2, 1770, [in BUCEM, in BL g.421.d.(1.)]
Was this also issued earlier by Kammel himself, making Welcker edition a reissue? Would make better sense if this was the case.

A Second Sett of Six Sonatas for Two Violins and a Bass, Op.3, 1769, [in BUCEM, in BL g.222.h.(1.)]
Either the first work by Kammel to be issued by Welcker, or the date is an error.

Six Quartettos for Two Violins a Tenor and Violoncello Obligato, Op.4, 1770, [in BUCEM, in BL g.411.(1), in BL R.M.16.f.14.(13.)]

Six Duetts for Two Violins, Op.5, 1770, [in BL g.421.d.(2.)]

Six Notturnos for Two Violins and a Bass, Op.6, 1772, [in BUCEM]
First edition published by Kammel himself, but lists Welcker as joint vendor

Six Notturnos for Two Violins and a Bass, Op.6, 1775, [in BL h.2900.(3.)]
This time published under Welcker's own imprint

Six Notturnos for Two Violins and a Bass, Op.7, 1775]

Six Dancing Minuetts, in Three Parts for Two Violins and a Bass, [no Op], 1775, [b.55.f]

A Second Sett of Six Quartettos for Two Violins a Tenor and Violoncello Obligato, Op.7, 1775, [in BUCEM, in BL g.276.a.(1.)]
Six Solos for the Violin with a Thorough Bass for the Harpsichord, Op.8, 1775, [in BUCEM]

Six Sonatas for the Pianoforte, Harpsichord or Harp with accompaniments for a Violin and Violoncello, Op.9, 1775, [in BL g.161.l.(5.), RM.26.c.1.(3.)]

Six Solos for the Violin with a Thorough Bass for the Harpsichord, Op.10, 1776, [in BL h.1909]

Six Overtures for Two Violins, Two Oboes or Flutes, Two French Horns, A Tenor and a Bass for the Harpsichord, Op.10, 1776, [in BUCEM, in BL g.474.a.(1.)]

Six overtures, in Eight Parts by the following composers, I. Stamitz, II. Vanhall, III. Mislevecheck, IV. Princess Royal of Saxony, V. Hayden, VI. Vanhall, the whole collected by Antonio Kammel (arrangement), [no Op.] 1773, [in BUCEM, in BL g.474.(7.)]

Overtures, in Eight Parts Op.10, 1781

A Third Sett of Trios or Ballo Consisting of Two Acts, [no Op.], 1774, [in BUCEM, in BL g.270.v.(2.)]

ROBERT WORNUM/ Glass-House-Street, near Burlington Gardens, 'St. Jacques'

Music seller and publisher of small books of dances, in 1777 moved to 42 Wigmore Street, listed, in the Musical Directory for 1794 as violin and violoncello maker. [Kidson pp.155-156].

Six Quatuors à deux Violons, Alto, et Violoncello Obligés, Op.4, 1775, [in BUCEM, in BL h.1909.b]

[Page references are to Frank Kidson: British Music Publishers, Printers and Engravers. London: W. E. Hill & Sons, 1900].

Kammel's works in music collections and libraries

Catalogues of private collections and libraries are not only a source of information about Kammel's published works, but also indicate his influence.

In the 18th century, musical scores or parts were bought from music shops or the composers themselves at their home address. Music publications were often bought by subscription.

Analysis of subscription lists shows[1] a wide range of social categories among subscribers. They were not just members of the aristocracy, but also merchants, lawyers, musicians or entrepreneurs in music, and some were related to the composer. Musical societies, schools of music and other places of learning were also on the subscription lists.

What was the motivation of the people who bought music or subscribed for it? Some were collectors, some bought the music as a form of charity, some bought music in bulk for business and resold it. Some people put their name on the subscription lists to be seen in the company of the nobility. And finally, musicians bought the scores and parts for study and performance.

Kammel's works in private collections

Charles Burney's library

The British Library has a photographic reproduction of the original 1814 sale catalogue of the Burney collection from, complete with manuscript annotations and giving the prices paid for various items.[2]

It contains no manuscripts by Kammel at all, no lots devoted to Kammel's published works or listing Kammel as the main object of interest. Those

---

[1] Rasch, Rudolf. *Music publishing in Europe 1600-1900: concepts and issues bibliography.* BWV Berlin 2005

[2] White, John. *Catalogue of the Music Library of Charles Burney, Sold in London, 8 August 1814.* With an introduction by A. Hyatt King. Amsterdam: Fritz Knuf, 1973.

of Kammel's published works which are offered in the catalogue are included as make-weights to pad out selections of works by other composers:

757. Hachmeister's Minuet... -- Jerigs 12 Sonatas for Harpsichord -- Kammel's Sonatas, Op.9... [etc.]. Sold for 10s., together with lot 756.

765. Kalktrenner's Sonatas, Op.1 and 2 -- Kammel's do. Op.9 --Kohaut's do... [etc.].

766. King (M. P.) Sonatas, Op.1 and 2 -- Kammel's do. Op.9 -- 6 lessons by a lady... [etc.]

Lots 765 and 766 together sold for 2s 6d.

Thus, bizarrely, Burney seems to have owned three copies of Kammel's Op.9, and no other works! By 1814 Kammel's works were obviously judged to be almost worthless - see the composers with whom he is listed, and the low prices paid.

In view of this it is not likely Burney was a friend or supporter of Kammel!

Moffat music library

The Hirsch collection in the British Library has a catalogue of the sale of the Moffat collection:[3]

Kammel works are in lots nos.375-381.

375. *Six Sonatas Pour le Violon Avec la Basse Continue.* Oeuvre Neuvieme. A la Haye, B. Hummel, c.1765. Moffat's note says: 'Not in the British Museum'. The date seems rather early: predates the first publication of his Op.1 in London. The British Library catalogue estimates the date at 1775. The opus number does not match the numbering of his works in England where Op.9 is a set of piano sonatas.

376. *Six Notturnos a Deux Violons et Basse.* Oeuvre 6. Amsterdam, S. Markordt, c.1770. Moffat's note says: 'This is the original edition with the dedication to Mademoiselle Young de Delaford. Both Welcker and

---

[3] *The Valuable Music Library Formed by Alfred Moffat, Esq.* Otto Haas, 49a Belsize Park Gardens, London, N.W.3. [BL Hirsch 466]

Longman & Broderip published editions but without 'Dedication'. The latter is in the Brit. Museum but not the original Amsterdam edition'. Moffat seems unaware of the self-published London edition, c.1772. The assertion that the first edition was published in Amsterdam, however, is interesting, and if Kammel was in the habit of publishing early editions of some of his works abroad, this might help to explain why the dates of his early London publications are so irregular, cf. lot 381 below.

377. *Six Divertimentos for the Harpsichord or Piano-Forte Dedicated to Lady Banks.* London, J. Preston, c.1776. Moffat says: 'This is a very early Preston publication. Not in the British Museum'. The British Library catalogue estimates the date as 1783, which is probably too late. Moffat's ms. notes indicate 1776-78, of which the latter date is more plausible.

378. *Six Duettos for Two Violins.* Op. XVIII. London, at Kerpen's Music Shop, c.1776. Moffat says: 'The title pages of both parts bear Kammel's signature. Kerpen was unknown to Kidson. Not in the British Museum' The attributed date may be too early? The British Library catalogue gives the date as 1782 which tallies better with the position of this opus number in the sequence.

379. *Six Duets for Two Violins.* Opera 5th. London, the Author, and sold at his House, c.1768. Moffat says: 'With the old labels from the original covers inserted. This is the first issue of Kammel's Op.5, sold at his private address. Welcker put out a later edition: the latter is in the Museum but not the original Half-Moon Street publication'. Moffat's attributed date is too early: Kammel did not move to Half-Moon Street until c.1770.

380. *Sei Trii di Violino e Basso.* Opera Prima. 1766. Moffat says: 'The title-page is ornamental, headed with coat of arms and without publisher's name'. This is probably the self-published first edition.

381. *Six Sonates a Deux Violons.* Opera II. A La Haye, B. Hummel, 'On peut les avoir a Amsterdam chez J. J. Hummel', c.1767. Could this be the first edition, predating British printings? This would account for the muddle in dates. However, the British Library catalogue dates it 1775.

Kammel's works in subscription libraries

In the latter half of the 18th century, musical scores and parts were made available for loan in commercial subscription libraries.

Kammel's works in British libraries today

The holdings of the main library collections in Britain are listed in BUCEM and COPAC.[4]

According to these two listings the largest number (53) of Kammel's works is in the British Library. The second largest (21) is at the King's College Library, Cambridge. The Bodleian has 15; the Royal Academy 12; the Cambridge University 6; Glasgow University 5; Trinity College Dublin 4; the Aberdeen University, the London University, the Pendlebury Library Cambridge, the Henry Watson Music Library Manchester 3 each; the Bristol Library, Reid Library, Sheffield University, Southampton University 2 each; the Durham University, Royal College of Music and, Leeds University, the Shakespeare Memorial Library, 1 each.

Some of Kammel's works are not available at all, others have survived in multiple copies.

University of Aberdeen

Six trios for two violins and a violoncello, with a thorough bass for harpsichord, Op.16, J. Preston [c.1785] London

The library has only one work, published in the 18th century.

It arrived in the Library at Michaelmas (29 September) 1780, with Kammel's "Six Duetts" which have since gone missing. These two pieces of music by Kammel were sent by Stationers' Hall in London as part of a regular consignment of copyright material - to which the Library was entitled at that time. There is no related correspondence.[5]

---

[4] Schnapper b. Ed. *The British Union Catalogue of early music printed before 1801*. 2v. London: Butterworths Scientific Publications 1957; copac.ac.uk
[5] Early printed music is documented in Barry Cooper's "Catalogue of early printed music in Aberdeen libraries", *Research chronicle* v.14, 1978, pp.2-138, with special reference to pp.55-6. The item by Kammel is in Box 1 of the Stationers' Hall Music Collection which is being catalogued. There is also an article by Richard Turbet entitled "Music deposited by

Cambridge University

A second sett of six quartettos for two violins. a tenor and violoncello obligato, Op.7, P. Welcker [1775] London

Six divertimentos for the harpsichord or piano-forte, Op.17, J. Preston [c.1783] London

Op.7 was a gift to the library from the collection of **J. E. Nixon** of King's College.

King's College Cambridge

Sei trii, di violino e basso, Op.1, [1766] London

Sei trii, di violino e basso, Op.1, P. Welcker [1770] London

Sei trii, di violino e basso, Op.1, Thompson [1780] London

Six duets for two violins, Op.2, Welcker [ ] London

A second sett of six sonatas for two violins and a bass, Op.3, Welcker [1769] London

Six quartettos for two violins, a tenor and Violoncello obligato, Op.4, Welcker [ ] London

Six overtures in Eight Parts by the following composers, I. Stamitz, II. Vanhall, III. Mislevecheck, IV. Princess Royal of Saxony, V. Hayden, VI. Vanhall, the whole collected by Antonio Kammel (arrangement), S. A. & P. Thompson [c.1790] London

Six notturnos for two violins and a bass, Op.6, Self [c.1772] London

Six notturnos a deux violons et basse, Op.6, Markordt [ ] Amsterdam **[stamped T. Crompton]**

Six notturnos for two violins and a bass, Op.6, Longman & Broderip [c.1780] London **[name John Huley stamped on t.p.]**

Stationers' Hall at the Library of the University and King's College of Aberdeen, 1753-96", *Research chronicle* v.30, 1997, pp.139-62, especially p.142.

Six notturnos a deux violons et basse, Op.6, Welcker [ ] London

A third sett of trios or ballo consisting of two acts, Welcker [c.1774] London

Six sonates a deux violons et basse, Op.7, B. Hummel [c.1775] Haag

A second sett of six quartettos for two violins, a tenor and violoncello obligato, Op.7, P. Welcker [1775] London

Six solos for the violin with a thorough bass for the harpsichord, Op.8, Welcker [c.1775] London

Six solos for the violin with a thorough bass for the harpsichord, Op.8 John Preston [c.1785] London

Six divertimentos pour deux violons ou violon et alto viola, Op.17, J. Schmidt [c.1790] Amsterdam

Six duettos for two violins, Op.18, Kerpen [1782], engr. by T. Straight London

Six notturnos for two violins and violoncello, Op.19, Self [ ] London

Six sonatas for two violins and a violoncello with thorough bass for the harpsichord, by Bach, Abel and Kammel, Welcker [c.1775] London

The majority of these works in the King's College were part of the collection of the noted bibliophile, **Louis Thompson Rowe**, which was given to the library by an anonymous benefactor who purchased his collection in 1928. Of the few that do not appear to have come from Rowe's collection, there is little to indicate their provenance apart from a couple of names stamped on title pages. Charles Henry Vincent Pixell was associated with the Hymns Ancient and Modern. In 1759 John Pixell published a collection of songs.

Pendlebury Library of Music Cambridge

A second sett of six sonatas for two violins and a bass, Op.3, P. Welcker [1769] London

Sei trii, di violino e basso, Op.1, P. Welcker [1770] London

Six notturnos for two violins and a bass, Op.6, P. Welcker [1772] London

The publications were acquired probably at some point in the twentieth century. The inside cover of "Sei trii" has the inscription "**George Molineux Montgomerie**", the "Six notturnos" has the inscription of "**G. R. G. Ricketts**, Christ Church, Oxford" and the library book plate with "presented by **Miss J. Palmer**".

George Molineux Montgomerie (1869-1915) was Major of the Grenadier Guards.

Reid Music Library, Edinburgh University Library

Six notturnos for two violins and violoncello, Op.19, J. Welcker [c1785] London

Six divertimentos, as quartets, three for two violins, a tenor and violoncello, and three for a German flute or hautboy, two violins and violoncello, Op.12, Walker [1800] London

The library has no information about the provenance of these two works.

Glasgow University

Six duetts, four for two violins, and two for a violin and tenor, Op.15, J. Preston [c.1785] London

Six duetts, four for two violins, and two for a violin and tenor, Op.15, J. Preston [1800] London

Six trios for two violins and a violoncello, with a thorough bass for harpsichord, Op.16, J. Preston [c.1785] London

The library has no information about the provenance of these two works.

Henry Watson Music Library Manchester

Sei trii, di violino e basso, Op.1, S. A. & P. Thompson [1780] London

Six quartettos for two violins, a tenor and violoncello obligato, Op.4, P. Welcker [1770] London

A second sett of six quartettos for two violins a tenor and violoncello obligato, Op.7, P. Welcker [1775] London

The library was formed in 1899 from a collection which began in 1860s. So the Kammel holdings will have been through several pairs of hands before they came to the library.

Bodleian Library Oxford

A second sett of six sonatas for two violins and a bass, Op.3, P. Welcker [1769] London, 2 copies

Sei trii, di violino e basso, Op.1, P. Welcker [1770] London, 2 copies

Six quartettos, Op.4, P. Welcker [1770] London

Six notturnos for two violins and a bass, Op.6, P. Welcker [1772] London

Six overtures, collected by A. Kammel, Welcker [1773] London

Six sonatas for the pianoforte, Op.9, Welcker [1776] London

Six duettos, Op.11, Longman & Broderip [c.1780] London

Six duetts, four for two violins, and two for a violin and tenor, Op.15, J. Preston [c.1785] London

Six duetts, four for two violins, and two for a violin and tenor, Op.15, J. Preston [c.1794] London

Six trios for two violins and a violoncello, with a thorough bass for harpsichord, Op.16, J. Preston [c.1785] London

Two works - Op.15 and 16 - were acquired under copyright deposit. Two came from the **Lord Leigh** collection, and one from the collection of

Henry Dashwood (Six overtures 1773). Three were 20th century acquisitions.

The names inscribed in some of these compositions are: "**Robert Collet Payne, September 28th 1805**" (Op.11), and "**Harriet Anne Southwell 1776**" (Op.9).

Shakespeare Centre Library, Stratford

Six dancing minuets in three parts for two violins and a bass, J. Welcker [c.1775] London

It is bound with five other pamphlets of contemporary minuets. The name of probably a nineteenth century owner is "**C. H. Hutchinson**". One of the pamphlets, dated 1765, has a contemporary owner's name on its title page, "**R. Richmond**".

Owners of Kammel's published music

T. Crompton

His name is stamped on *Six notturnos a deux violons et basse*, Op.6, Markordt [ ] Amsterdam, in King's College Cambridge

Henry Dashwood

Six overtures, collected by A. Kammel, Welcker [1773] London, in the Bodleian Library, came from the 18th century collection of Henry Dashwood.

George Henry Dashwood, Esq. was a MP for Buckinghamshire in 1837 and 1841.

According to the 1841 census, Henry Dashwood, born about 1821, lived with his parents Sir George Dashwood, born about 1791, and Lady Dashwood in St. Marylebone.

John Huley

His name is stamped on the title page of *Six notturnos for two violins and a bass*, Op.6, Longman & Broderip [c.1780] London, in King's College Cambridge.

C. H. Hutchinson

In the Shakespeare Centre Library at Stratford, Kammel's composition *Six dancing minuets in three parts for two violins and a bass,* J. Welcker [c.1775] London, was probably owned by C. H. Hutchinson.

Lord Leigh

Two of Kammel's compositions in the Bodleian Library Oxford - *A second sett of six sonatas for two violins and a bass,* Op.3, P. Welcker [1769] London; and *Six notturnos for two violins and a bass,* Op.6, P. Welcker [1772] London, came from the Lord Leith 18th Century Collection.

George Molineux Montgomerie

His name is inscribed on the inner cover of *Sei trii, di violino e basso,* Op.1, P. Welcker [1770] London, at the Pendelbury Library Cambridge.

According to the census of 1841 he was a clergyman in Norfolk. He was born about 1796 and lived with his married daughter Mary born about 1806 and her husband Henry Goldsmith born about 1811.

J. E. Nixon of King's College

A second sett of six quartettos for two violins a tenor and violoncello obligato, Op.7, P. Welcker [1775] London, donated to the Cambridge University Library from his collection.

Miss J. Palmer

The book-plate of *Six notturnos for two violins and a bass,* Op.6, P. Welcker [1772] London, in the Pendlebury Library Cambridge, says "Presented by Miss J. Palmer".

Robert Collet Payne

Six duettos, Op.11, Longman & Broderip [c1780] London in the Bodleian Library Oxford, is inscribed "Robert Collet Payne, Sept 28th 1805".

Charles Pixell

His name appears in *Six duettos for two violins,* Op.18, Kerpen [1782], engr. by T. Straight London, in King's College Cambridge.

Charles Henry Vincent Pixell was associated with the Hymns Ancient and Modern. In 1759 John Pixell published a collection of songs.

R. Richmond

In the Shakespeare Centre Library at Stratford, Kammel's composition *Six dancing minuets in three parts for two violins and a bass,* J. Welcker

138

[c.1775] London, is bound with five other pamphlets of contemporary minuets. One of the pamphlets dated 1765 has a contemporary owner's name on its title page "R. Richmond".

G. R. G. Ricketts
His name is inscribed in *Six notturnos for two violins and a bass*, Op.6, P. Welcker [1772] London, in the Pendlebury Library Cambridge.

Louis Thompson Rowe
The original owner of the majority of Kammel's compositions in King's College Cambridge. They were given to the library by an anonymous benefactor who had purchased Rowe's collection in 1928.

Harriet Anne Southwell
Six sonatas for the pianoforte, Op.9, Welcker [1776] London, in the Bodleian Library Oxford is inscribed "Harriet Anne Southwell 1776".

APPENDIX V

Anthony Kammel's descendants

Lucy (1769 Stratford Saye-**1770** St. Marylebone**)**
William (1770 Westminster- **?)**
Elizabeth Rosina (1772 Westminster-**1846** Cheam**)**
  x Edward William Gilbert 1793 Holborn
  Edward George Antonio Gilbert (1794 Holborn-**?)**
    x Tabitha Hosier 1824 Holborn/City?
    Tabitha Gilbert (1826 Newington – **1889** St. Giles**)**
      x Richard Limpus 1848 Camberwell
    Edward Gilbert (1824 Newington – **1880** St. Giles**)**
      x Caroline Mary Sale 1866 Pancras
      Newton Edward Sale Gilbert (1868 Penge – **1916** Headington**)**
      Erasmus James Denby Gilbert (1869 Penge – **1923** Steyning**)**
      Caroline Mary Gilbert (1870 Holborn – **1870** Holborn**)**
    Matilda Gilbert (1832 Newington – **1907** Kensington**)**
      x William T Snosswell 1866 Whitechapel
      x Mathias Erasmus Wesley 1879 Holborn
Thomas Gilbert (1795 Westminster- **?)**
Joseph Gilbert (1799 Holborn- **?)**
  ?x Rebecca Shambrook 1824 Southwark
x James Brown 1804 Westminster
James Henry Brown (1805 Southwark- **?)**
  ?x Sarah Elizabeth Mills 1829 City
  ?x Mary
Elizabeth Brown (1807 Southwark - **?1808)**
Mary Brown (1808 Southwark - **?)**
Eliza Brown (1809 Southwark – **1887** Epsom**)**
  x James Dixon Baker 1831 Newington
  James Baker (1831? Ewell - **1963?)**
    ?x Ann?
    Louisa Baker (1852 Ewell - **?** before **1911)**
      x Thomas Henry Ditch in 1875 d.1922 Westminster
      Lucy Agnes Ditch (1876 - ?)
        x Walter Tidmarsh 1894 Newington
        Lucy Tidmarsh (1897 Wandsworth **? - ?)**
        Louie Tidmarsh (1899 Wandsworth **? - ?)**
      Caroline Sarah Ditch (1880 Lambeth **?)**
        x George Jones 1899 Southwark
        Caroline Ethel Jones (1900 Southwark – **1963** Chichester?**)**
        Dorothy Blanche Jones (1901 Brixton - **?)**
        William Thomas Jones (1905 Brixton - **?)**
        Albert Charles Jones (1906 Brixton - **?)**
      Thomas Ditch (1882 – Wandsworth **1951?)**
      Charles Ditch (1885 – Lambeth - **?)**
        x Ellen betw. 1902-1911

Joseph John [Topher?] Ditch (1886 Lambeth - **?)**
   x Elizabeth M. Champ 1913 Wandsworth
Leonora Ditch (1888 Lambeth - **?)**
Clara Ditch (1891 Lambeth – **1935** Wandsworth)
   Guildford   x Alfred John Gray 1911 Newington
    Alfred John Gray (1912 Southwark - **?)**
Elizabeth Ditch (1893 Lambeth - **?)**
   x George T. Vowles 1915 Wandsworth
Ivy F. Vowles [f. George T. m. Elizabeth] (1918 Wandsworth - **?)**
Bessie L. Vowles [f. George T. m. Elizabeth] (1918 – Wandsworth - **?)**
James Joseph Baker (1853 Ewell – **1917** Ewell)
Thomas Baker (1855 Ewell - **?)**
John Baker (1857 Ewell - **?)**
Robert Baker (1860 Ewell - **?)**
William James Baker (1863 Ewell - **?)**
John Baker (1833 Ewell – **1841** Epsom)
Rachel Baker (1835 Ewell - **?)**
Thomas Simms Baker (1837 Ewell - **?)**
George Baker (1839 Ewell - **?)**
Eliza Baker (1841 Ewell - **?)**
   x Robert Chandler 1872 Albury, Surrey
   Henry Chandler (1873 Guildford - **?)**
      x Florence Jane/Julia? 1900
      Henry Frederick Chandler (1900 Guildford- **?)**
      Florence Emma Chandler (1901 Chertsey - **?)**
      Frank Chandler (1908 Walton - **?)**
   Louisa Jane Chandler (1908 Hambledon, Surry - **?)**
      x George Harrington 1891 Camberwell
   William Alfred Chandler (1876 Hambledon, Surrey - **?)**
      x Selina Ann Crane 1899 Southwark
      Alfred H. Chandler (1900 Southwark – **1987** Surrey SE?**)**
      Albert J. Crane Chandler (1890 Southwark - **?) adopted**
      x Edith Mary Walker 1908
      William Alexander Chandler (1903 Wandsworth – **1967** Sutton)
   Rose Chandler (1878 Hambledon, Surry - **?)**
      Albert Chandler (1897 Walton - **?)**
   Lily Chandler (1878 Hambledon – **1888** Southwark)
   Annie Chandler (1880 Hambledon – **1909)**
      x Arthur Harry Watson, Southwark 1901
   Ethel Chandler (1883 Hambledon - **?)**
   Eliza Chandler (1885 Hambledon - **?)**
      X Ian Emery Epsom 1907?
   Minnie Chandler (1886 Hambledon - **?)**
   Robert Chandler (1891 Hambledon - **?)**
William Charles Baker (1845 Ewell - **?)**
   x Emma Ann Penfold ?
   x Mary Ann Thoms nee Penfold, Kingston 1890
   Albert Edward Baker (1896 Mitcham - **?)**
   x Hannah Baker ?
Mary Ann Baker (1847 Ewell - **?)**

Sarah Ann Baker (1854 Ewell – **1898** Ewell)
?Amey Brown (1811 Southwark - **?)**
    ?Harriet Brown (1813 Southwark - **?)**
    ?John Brown (1816 Southwark – **1850?)**
Marcia Mary (1774 Westminster - **?)**
George Anthony (1775 Westminster – **1828?** St Pancras)
Henry Christian John (1777 Westminster – **1821** Soho)
    x Patty Sophia Searle 1799 Cripplegate
    Elizabeth Ann Camels (1800 Cripplegate - **?)**
    ?x Martha ? Westminster ?
    George Antonio Kammell (1806 Westminster - **?)**
    Elizabeth Ann Kammell (1811 Soho - **?)**
Horace Christopher (1779 Westminster - **?)**
Henry James (1780 Westminster - **?)**
    ?x Rebecca
        ?Henry Cammall (1816 Finsbury - **?)**
        ?Henry Cammall (1817 Cripplegate - **?)**
    ?x Elizabeth
        ?Mary Ann Cammell (1818 Westminster - **?)**
        ?Susana Cammell (1818 Westminster - **?)**

APPENDIX VI

Who was who in Kammel's life

Who was who - AB

Karl Friedrich Abel (1723-1787) came to London in 1763 and he obtained denization in 1775. His mother and her sister joined him in London where they both died in 1766.[1] He lived with Bach in Meard Street until 1771 when he moved out. Later he lived with a watch maker Mr. Herve in Greek Street, and finally with William Cramer in Carlisle Street, in 201 Oxford Street and in 6 Duke Street. He was very close to Bach. After Bach's death in 1782 he went to Germany, but returned to his house in Duke Street in 1785 and carried on with playing at concerts. He died in 1787.

The main patron of the Bach and Abel's concerts was **Willoughby Bertie, 4th Earl of Abingdon** (1740-1799). He provided a substantial proportion of the funding for the concerts. He was a composer and a friend of Haydn. He lived in Upper Brook Street.

Who was who – AN

Thomas Anson (1695-1773) MP for Litchfield, of St. James Square. In 1770 Kammel dedicated his Op.5 to him. He was elected 1761, married in 1767 and died in 1773.

Kammel was a composer in residence at Thomas Anson's seat at Shugborough.

He performed at a Thomas Anson's series of Breakfast Concerts at his London House, 15 St. James Square. James Harris of Salisbury wrote that Thomas Anson's concerts featured "the best hands in London" and at Thomas's death wrote: 'All his friends were sharers of his most elegant entertainments.'

In his Will Thomas Anson left Anthony Kammel an annuity of £50

---

[1] *The Gentleman's Magazine*, 1763 Deaths 14 March 1766

Who was who – AY

Earl of Aylesford, (1751-1780) Heneage Finch, of Grosvenor Square. He was born in 1751 at Sion House, Isleworth and died 1821 at Gt. Packington in Warwickshire. In 1780 Kammel dedicated his Op.15 to him.

Who was who - BA

Johann Christian Bach (1735-1782) came to London in 1763. He lived in Meard Street, Queen Street and Carlisle Street. He married the famous singer Galli who, according to Mrs. Papendiek "assisted him with her savings of £2,000".[2] He died in 1782.

Benjamin Banks (1727-1750) was a violin maker in Salisbury. Kammel used to take part in the Salisbury Festivals. Kammel must have known him as Blake's daughter Anne visited Kammel in London.[3]

Who was who – BA

Lady Banks, to whom Kammel dedicated Op.13 in 1778 and Op.17 in 1781, was most likely Lady Dorothea Banks (1782-1828), wife of Sir Joseph Banks. They belonged to the Church of the Moravian Brethren. Kammel, however, was not a member of the Church.[4] Sir Joseph Banks had a sister, Sophia Sarah Banks. He lived at 32 Soho Square and had a house in Kent called Provender very near to Norton Court, where Kammel is probably buried.[5]

Who was who - BE

Charles Christian Besser, his brother-in-law from Germany. He was an executor of Kammel's Will. He was a German merchant. His address in Germany is not known.

J. Betz of 21 Rupert Street was a music seller, publisher and importer of foreign music. In 1780 he published a French reissue of Kammel's Op.9.

George Betts (1755-1823) was a violin maker. In 1818 he was a

---

[2] Papendiek, Charlotte Louisa Henrietta (1887) .v.1 p.109
[3] Burrows, Donald & Dunhill, Rosemary (2001) p.1030
[4] According to the Moravian library [17 September 1992]
[5] Heal, Ambrose. *London Tradesman's cards of the 18th century*. Batsford, 1925 p.27

witness at the marriage of John Cammell, who may have been one of Anthony Kammel's sons.

Who was who - BL

Benjamin Blake (1750-1827), a violinist. He was born in 1750 or 1751 in Kingsland, Hackney. He studied with Kammel and Cramer and became a member of the King's Theatre Orchestra. He lived in Manchester Street. In 1793 he taught at the Camden House boarding school Kensington.

Who was who – BO

William Boyce (1710-1779) was Master of the King's Band. He was associated with the Salisbury Festival and probably arranged for Kammel to lead the orchestra.

Who was who - BR

Broderip & Longman were music publishers at 13 Haymarket and also at The Harp & Crown, 26 Cheapside. In 1780 they published reissues of Kammel's Op.3 and Op.6.

Who was who - CA

John Caulfield was a music engraver at 5 Piccadilly. In 1780 he printed Kammel's Op.14.

Who was who - CR

William Cramer (1746-1799) came to London in 1772. He lived with Abel in Queen Street in the 1770s and in no.201 Oxford Street from 1776. He was a leader at the Salisbury Festival. He gave 8 London concerts with Kammel.

Who was who - JC

John Crosdill (1750-1825), a cellist and violist, was a member of the King's Band of Music, Chamber musician to Queen Charlotte, and cello teacher to the Prince of Wales. He was principal violoncello at the meetings of the Three Choirs at Gloucester 1769-1778. Miss Edicott sang at his benefice concerts in 1778 and 1779. He appeared in 13 London concerts with Kammel. ABC Dario Musico says that he "has risen to the highest perfection".[6]

He lived in Titchfield Street. In 1769 tickets for Kammel's concerts were sold at a corner of Gt. Titchfield Street, which could have been John Crosdill's residence. John Crosdill later moved to Grosvenor Square. His father's residence was in Nottingham Street. His father died in 1790. His friends were Lord Fitzwilliam and B. Thompson.

In 1785 he married a rich wife, Elizabeth Colebrooke, and retired from music. Various reference books have mistakenly stated that Kammel married a rich wife.

Who was who – DE

The **Duke of Devonshire** (1748-1811) William Cavendish, was the dedicatee of Kammel's Op.10 in 1775. The Duke was married to Georgiana nee Spencer to whom Kammel dedicated his Op.7 in 1775. She used to visit her relative, Mr. Poyntz of Midgham House in Newberry. Kammel dedicated his Six Dancing Minuets (without Opus number) in 1775 to "a select assembly at Newberry". The archivist of Chatsworth House says that there is no mention of Kammel in the Chatsworth archive.

Who was who - DO

Michael Donaghoe moved to no.34 Half Moon Street in April 1784. In a 1790 list of households he is described as a physician.[7]

Who was who - ED

Miss **Lydia Edicatt** was one of the younger sisters of Kammel's wife Anne.

Miss Edicatt sang at three Kammel benefit concerts: in 1778, 1779 and 1780.

During the five years between 1778 and 1783 she performed at 6 London concerts, mostly at the Tottenham Street Rooms. Her last concert took place at the Freemasons Hall on 10 March 1783. The

---

[6] *ABC Dario Musico* (1780) p.18
[7] In the Westminster Poll Book 1818, Parish of St. Martin, p.104:
"Donaghoo Thomas 15 Adam St Adelphi M.D."

review of her last concert, conducted by Solomon, was not very positive: "This lady seemed to be indisposed, and could not give a full scope to her vocal powers".[8]

Lydia Edicatt married a German merchant Charles Christian Besser on 1 April 1783, shortly after the last concert and left the musical scene.

Who was who - EL

Ann Elliott of Greek Street was a witness to Anthony Kammel's marriage in 1768. She died a year later. Presumably she was Kammel's landlady when he first came to London.

Who was who - FE

Fentnum, a music shop at 78 Strand, sold Kammel's music. Copies of reissues of Op.1 and Op.6 held by the British Library were purchased there.

Who was who - FI

John Christian Fischer (1733-1800) was an oboist who gave 17 concerts with Kammel. He came to London in 1770. He married Mary Gainsborough.

Who was who – FU

Mrs. Fuller moved to no.34 Half Moon Street in February 1786. A note in the rate-book says: "Anthony Kammel - Tenant no.34 – Mrs. Fuller". In September 1786 there is a note "Mrs. Fuller moved away from no.34 Half Moon Street". In 1791 and 1793 Rose Fuller Esq. is recorded as living in no.18 Wigmore Street.

Who was who - GR

Greenwood was an auctioneer at Leicester Square.

Who was who - HA

Francis Hackwood (-   ), a violinist. After his marriage in 1768 to Isabella Donaldson he lived in 10 Half Moon Street between 1768 and

---

[8] *Morning Post* 11 March 1783

1781. In 1782 he joined the King's Band and moved to no.35 Half Moon Street, next door to Anthony Kammel. He was described by a contemporary as "eccentric, whimsical, mean, well known by the nobility".[9]

James Harris (1709-1780) was a philosopher and musical entrepreneur in Salisbury. He was another patron of Anson's friend Anton Kammel. His letters mention a whole series of concerts at 15 St. James Square where 'the best hands in London' (including Kammell) could be found.

John Hayward paid £175 to Kammel on 30 May 1780. Between the years 1785 and 1796 John Howard is listed as a stock-broker in Oxford Street, Black Swan Street.

Who was who - HI

Edward & Milicent Hitchings of St. Marylebone, were witnesses to Ann Kammel's marriage in 1787 to Richard Tanner. The 1787 rate books for Marylebone do not list the name of Hitchings. Edward Hitchings married Milicent Rawson at Marylebone in 1787. In 1795 Edward Hitchings was buried in the Bunnhill Fields Cemetery.

Who was who – HO

John Hoper paid £200 to Kammel on 25 June 1778. John Hoper was vicar of Steyning, Head of the Steyning Grammar School and rector of Piccombe. There was also a builder called John Hooper who did work for Kammel's friend Thomas Anson in Shugborough.

Who was who - KE

Kerpen's music shop in 19 Wardour Street was a vendor and/or publisher of Kammel's Op.18 in 1782.

Who was who - LI

William Lindeman (1742-   ) of 459 Strand. He was born in the City in 1742, married Elizabeth Stent in 1764 in St. Martin in the Fields. After 1774 he paid rates at Westminster for no.459 Strand. By profession he

---

[9] Park, William Thomas. *Musical memoirs* 2v, London, 1830, v.1, p.103

was an oilman. In 1784 he was a witness to Kammel's Will.[10]

Who was who - MA

Lady Lucy Mann (1737-1778) Kammel's very first published composition in 1766 was dedicated to her with the words: "La prima e la principale mia protettrice al mio comparire in questa capitale". Sir Horace Mann 1st Bt a British representative in Florence had a nephew called also Horatio Mann 2nd Bt. The nephew married Lucy Noel in 1765 and they had a daughter called Lucy christened 2 April 1766 in St. James West.

Sir Horatio had his family seat at Bourn, near where Kammel was possibly buried. Within its grounds he had his own cricket ground, Bishopbourne Paddock.

Massinghi's Italian Warehouse in Dover Street sold Kammel's Op.5 in 1770.

Who was who - NO

Henry Noel was a witness to the marriage of Charles Besser and Lydia Edicatt in 1783. Henry Noel 6th Earl of Gainsborough and Baron Noel of Titchfield (1743-1798) lived in Harley Street, Cavendish Square and Princes Street. He was a relative of Lucy Mann. He could have been the "Mr. Nouelle" with whom Kammel had travelled incognito in 1766.[11]

Who was who - OB

Joseph Obermayer (1749-   ), a violinist. He is said to have studied with Kammel in Bohemia.

Who was who – OT

Richard Ottley and **Miss Ottley** were dedicatees of Kammel's two compositions, Op.8 and Op.9, in 1775.

Richard Ottley (1730-1775), the eldest son of Drewry Ottley, was born in St. Christophers, some time of Dunstan Park, Thatcham, Berkshire, lived

---

[10] In the British Library manuscript department there are letters of William Lindeman to J. Caryll [Add. 28232, f.387. Add. 28233, f.306. Add. 28234, ff. 46, 90, 177].
[11] Fremanová, Michaela (2001)

in Argyll Street, St. James, Westminster. In 1770 he married Sarah Elizabeth Young in Iver, Buckinghamshire. He owned estates in St. Vincent and in Tobago. His son Drewry Ottley (1755-1805) was President and Chief Justice of St. Vincent. One of Drewry's sons was Sir Richard Ottley (1782-1845), born in St. Vincent, Chief Justice of Grenada in 1814, and later of Ceylon, was knighted by King George IV at Carlton House on 22 March 1820.

Who was who – PA

Sir Gregory Page Turner (1748-1805) MP for Thirsk, of Portland Place was the dedicatee of Kammel's Op.14 in 1780. In the 1841 Census for St. Marylebone he is described as Independent and his birth given as about 1791.

His early 18th Century ancestor, **Sir Gregory Page**, second and last baronet spent a large part of his fortune on the purchase of the vast estate of Wricklemarch in Blackheath in 1725. He pulled down the old manor house and built what fifty years later was described as "the first habitable house in the Kingdom" at the cost of £90,000. On his death without issue in 1775 he bequeathed everything to his great-nephew Sir Gregory **Turner** who added Page to his surname.

Mrs Papendiek
Assistant-Keeper of the Wardrobe and Reader to Her Majesty.

Who was who – PI

In 1770 Kammel dedicated his Op.4 to **George Pitt** (1721-1803).

Kammel's daughter Lucy was born at Stratfield Saye where the Pitt family resided at Stratfield Saye House. Between the years 1761 and 1768 George Pitt was envoy to the count of Turin. Did he meet Kammel in Italy?

Who was who - PR

John Preston of 105 (later 97) Strand, published Kammel's Six divertimentos for a harpsichord (without opus number).

Who was who - RA

Robert Rawlings (Rawlins) (1742-1814), a violinist, travelled Europe for

9 years with the Duke of York as his musical page until 1767. He could have met Anthony Kammel on his travels. On his return to England he became a violinist in the King's and Queen's bands. Possibly he was the musician for whom Kammel substituted.

His son Thomas Augustus (1774-1849) was a violinist and composer.

Who was who - RE

Charles & Thomas Reeve of 32 Half Moon Street. They were Kammel's neighbours and close friends. Charles was described in a census as "window tax collector, local dealer". In 1767 the rates were paid by **William Reeve** who was presumably their father. Thomas was a witness to Kammel's Will, Charles was an executor.

Charles Reeve paid rates in Half Moon Street between 1782 and 1785. In 1790 he is listed as having a business at no.34. He was a coal dealer. He was an executor of Kammel's Will.

William Reeve paid rates at Half Moon Street in 1767.

Who was who – SO

John Cochrane Sole (-1790), to whom Kammel dedicated Op.16 in 1780, was an educated man who lived at Havering Bower near Romford and later in North Court near Faversham.

It is possible that Kammel was staying with him when he died as he is very likely buried in St. Mary Norton. After Sole's death his daughter auctioned his valuables, among them "a capital violin which formerly belonged to the celebrated Kammel."

Who was who - ST

Benjamin Starling of James Street, Covent Garden. He married in 1778 in Enfield and lived in James Street, Covent Garden. He was an executor of Kammel's Will.

Thomas Stanton paid £200 to Kammel on 5 August 1777. There were several people of this name and it is difficult to decide who it was and why he paid Kammel such a large sum of money.

Who was who - TE

Giusto Ferdinando Tenducci, (1735-1790), soprano castrato and composer gave 5 London concerts with Kammel.

Henry Roper Baron of Teynham, Peer in the county of Kent. Probably the 11th Baron (1734-1786)

Who was who - TH

Thompson of St. Paul's Churchyard published a reissue of Kammel's Op.2 in 1778 and Op.1 in 1780.

Who was who – WA

Count Vincent of Waldstein was Anthony Kammel's chief protector in his native country of Bohemia. Kammel dedicated his Op.3 to him in 1769.

Who was who - WE

Karl Weiss (1735-1795). In 1760 Weiss accompanied an English nobleman to Rome and afterwards came to London. Was a principal flutist in the King's Band. He gave 6 London concerts with Kammel. He lived at Queen Ann Street. His son Charles, born 1777, was also a flutist.

Peter & Mary Welcker of 10 Haymarket were Kammel's main publishers. In 1769 they published Op.3, in 1770 Op.2, Op.4 and a reissue of Op.1, in 1772 they were a joint vendors of Op.6, in 1773 they published Six overtures (without opus number), in 1775 Op.7, Op.8 and a reissue Op.6, in 1776 Op.10.

Their son **John Welcker** at 80 Haymarket published Kammel's Op.9 and his Six dancing minuets (without opus number) in 1775, and Six sonatas by Abel/Bach/Kammell in 1777.

Who was who - WO

Lady Worgden is listed in the rate-books under no.34 Half Moon Street. In 1769 there is a note "empty two quarters", in 1770 "Empty 2 quarters, Anth. J. Mr. Kammell".

R. Wornum of Glass House Street published a French reissue of Op.9.

Who was who - YO

Sir William Young was the dedicatee of Kammel's Op.19 in 1784, and **Lady Young of Delaford** of Kammel's Op.6 in 1772. Sir William Young, 2nd Bt (1749-1815) was a Governor of Tobago and a politician. His country seat was Hartwell in Buckinghamshire. The Buckinghamshire archive has a "Map of the estate of Sir William Young, bart called Delaford, surveyed by John Bellingham in 1770".

Who was who - ZA

Francesco Zappa was an Italian cellist and composer.

Publications which mention Kammel's name

ABC Dario Musico (1780).
Bath, 1780

Baker, Theodore (1900)
Baker's biographical dictionary of musicians, centennial edition, ed. By N. Slonimsky & L. Kuhn. New York: Schirmer, 2001

Burchell, Jenny (1996)
Polite or commercial concerts? Concert management and orchestral repertoire in Edinburgh, Bath, Oxford, Manchester and Newcastle 1730-1799. New York, London: Garland Publishing, 1996

Burrows Donald & Dunhill Rosemary (2001)
Music and theatre in Handel's world: The family papers of James Harris 1732-1780. Oxford: OUP, 2001

Capri, Antonio (1945)
Giuseppe Tartini. Milano: 1945

Carse, dam von Ahn (1940)
The orchestra in the XVIII century. Cambridge: Heffer, 1940

Choron, Alexandre Etien & Fayolle, Francois Joseph (1810)
Dictionnaire historique des musiciens. Reprinted Hildesheim; New York: George Olms Verlag, 1971

Cowgill, Rachel & Holman, Peter (2007)
Music in the British provinces 1690-1914. Aldershot: Ashgate, 2007

Cudworth, Charles L. (1958)
Antonín Kammel. In *Die Musik in Geschichte und Gegenwart* 1958, v.7 col.476-7

Dlabač, Jan Bohumír (1815)
Allgemeines historisches Künstler-Lexikon für Böhmen und zum Theil auch für Mähren und Schlesien. 2v Prague 1815

Eitner, Robert (1900)
Biographisch-bibliographisches Quellen-Lexikon der Musiker und Musikgelehrten der christlichen Zeitrechnung bis zur Mitte des neunzehnten Jahrhunderts. 10v Leipzig 1900-1904

Fetis, Francois Joseph (1898)
Biographie Universelle des Musiciens. In *Notes about Obermayer* v.4, p.472 about Kammel

Fischmann, Zdenka E. (2002)
Essays on Czech music. Boulder: East European Monographs, 2002

Forkel, Johann Nicolaus (1784)
Musikalischer Almanach für Deutschland auf das Jahr 1782-1784. Leipzig, 1781-1784

Freemanová Michaela, Pilková Zdeňka, Šimsová Sylva, Kuna Milan (1994)
K závěti Antonína Kammela. In *Hudební věda* v.31, no.2, 1994, pp.183-185

Freemanová, Michaela (1994)
Antonín Kammel v Londýně. In *Hudební věda* v.31, no.2, 1994, pp.399-402

Freemanová, Michaela (1999)
Korespondence Antonína Kammela a další dokumenty k životu a dílu českých hudebníků 18. Století, působících v Anglii, jako problém badatelský a etický. *In Kritické edice hudebních památek III.* Olomouc: Universita Palackého, 1999, pp.129-134

Freemanova Michaela (2001)
A certain Mr. Nouelle...: A Rutland Association for the Musician Anton Kammel. *Rutland Record* v.21, 2001, pp.35-39

Freemanová, Michaela (2003a)
Kammel, Antonín. In *Die Musik in Geschichte und Gegenwart.* ed. by Ludwig Finscher) 2nd ed. Kassel: Bärenreiter, 2003, pp.1431-1433

Freemanová, Michaela & Mikanová, Eva (2003b)
"My honourable Lord and Father...": 18th Century English Music through Bohemian Eyes. *Early Music*, v.31, no.2, 2003, pp.210-231

Gerber, Ernst Ludwig (1790)
Historisch-biographisches Lexicon der Tonkünstler Leipzig 1790. v.1. col.706

James, Kenneth Edward (1987)
Concert life in eighteenth-century Bath: A Thesis. Royal Holloway College, University of London, 1987

Knape, Walter (1973)
Karl Friedrich Abel. Bremen: Schünemann Universitätsverlag, 1973

McVeigh, Simon (1989)
The Violinist in London concert life 1750-1784. New York, London: Garland Publishing, 1989

McVeigh, Simon (2000)
Freemasonry and musical life in London in the late eighteenth century. In Jones, David Wynne, *Music in Eighteenth-century Britain*. Aldershot: Ashgate 2000, pp.72-100

Marsh, John (1998)
The John Marsh journals: the life and times of a gentleman composer (1752-1828) ed. by Brian Robins. New York: Pendragon Press 1998

Melville-Mason, Graham (1989)
The music and musicians of Bohemia and Moravia in Great Britain in the second half of the eighteenth and the early nineteenth centuries. In *Colloquium Musica ac societas (1740-1815)*. Brno: Filosofická fakulta MU, 1994, pp.101-108

Mikanová, Eva (1988)
Neznámá mozartovská bohemika. *Hudební rozhledy* v.16, no.4, 1988, pp.181-185

Mikanová, Eva (1989)
Valdštejnský úředník Antonín Kammel skladatelem v Anglii. In *Colloquium Musica ac societas (1740-1815)*, Brno: Filosofická fakulta MU, 1994, pp.139-144

Mozart, Wolfgang Amadeus (1776)
Mozart Briefe und Aufzeichnungen. Kassel: Bärenreiter, 1962, v.1. 1755-1776

Newmann, William S. (1963)
The Sonata in the classic era. Chapel Hill: The University of North Carolina Press, 1963, p.736

Papendiek, Charlotte Louisa Henrietta (1887)
Court and private life in the time of Queen Charlotte: being the journals of Mrs. Papendiek, Assistant-Keeper of the Wardrobe and Reader to Her Majesty. Edited by her granddaughter Mrs. V. D. Broughton. 2 vol. London: Bentley & Son, 1887

Pazdírek, Oldřich (1937)
Pazdírkův hudební slovník naučný. 2 vol. Brno: Pazdírek, 1937

Pilková, Zdeňka (1980)
Antonín Kammel. In *The New Grove dictionary of music and musicians.* London: Grove, v.9, 1980, pp.787-789.

Pilková, Zdeňka (1981)
Joseph Haydn and his Czech Contemporary Antonin Kammel. *Haydn Studies.* New York 1981, pp.171-177

Pilková, Zdeňka & Gerlach, Sonja (1982)
Sonata in A for Violin and Basso Continuo.
In *Boehmische Violinsonaten I.* Munchen: Henle Verlag, 1982

Pilková, Zdeňka (1984)
Kammel's Sinfonia in G and Sinfonia in D. In *The Symphony Series 1720-1840.* New York: Garland Publishing Inc., 1984, Series B, Vol.XIII, pp.25-87

Pilková, Zdeňka & Šimsová, Sylva (1993)
Nález závěti Antonína Kammela. In *Hudební věda*, 1993, v.4, pp.382-388

Pilková, Zdeňka & Šimsová, Sylva (1995)
The Will of Antonín Kammel. In *Czech Music* v.19, 1995-1996, pp.87-94

Pilková, Zdeňka (2001)
Kammel. In *The New Grove dictionary of music and musicians.* London: Grove, 2nd ed, 2001, v.13, pp.343-344

Pohl, Carl Ferdinand (1867)
Mozart und Haydn in London. New York: Da Capo Press, 1970

Portefeuille fur Musikliebhaber. (1792)
Berne, 1792

Poštolka, Milan (1961)
Josef Haydn a naše hudba 18. Století. Praha: Státní hudební vydavatelství, 1961

Racek, Jan (1958)
Česká hudba: od nejstarších dob do počátku 19. Století. Státní nakladatelství krázné literatury, hudby a umění, 1958

Riegger, Joseph Anton Stephan von (1787)
Materialen zur alten und neuen Statistik von Böhmen. XII Heft pp.243-244

Riemann, Carl Wilhelm Julus Hugo (1893)
Dictionary of music. London: Angener, 1893

Sainsbury (1824)
A dictionary of musicians from the earliest ages to the present time. 2 vol, London: Sainsbury, 1824

Straeten, Edmund Sebastian Joseph van der (1968)
The history of the violin: its ancestors and collateral instruments from earliest time. New York: Da Capo Press, 1968

Terry, Charles Stanford (1967)
John Christian Bach. Oxford: Oxford University Press, 1967

Wollenberg, Susan & McVeigh, Simon (2004)
Concert life in Eighteen-century Britain. Aldershot: Ashgate, 2004

APPENDIX VIII

Concise chronology

1765
K arrived
K met Mozart

1766
1 concert
1 publication
Dedicatee: Lucy Mann
Kent visit

1767
1 concert
Stamford concert

1768
3 concerts
London concert with Abel, Bach
Bath concert 2x
K marriage
Elliott Ann witness to marriage

1769
5 concerts
London concert with Abel, Bach, Brown, Cirri, Evans, Fedeli, Fischer 2x,
Gervasio, Giustinelli, Liutino, Merchi, Piatti, Siprutini, Weichsell, Weiss 2x
1 publication
Dedicatee: Waldstein
Bath concert
Stratfield Saye visit
K daughter born

1770
4 concerts
London concert with Abel, Bach. Brown. Evans, Fischer, Piece
Winchester concert
8 publications
Dedicatee: Anson, Pitt

K to Half Moon St
K son born

1771
3 concerts
London concert with Evans, Piece, Thomas, Weichsel
Salisbury concert

1772
4 concerts
London concert with Crosdill, Fischer, Sirmen
Salisbury concert
Shughborough concert
1 publication
Dedicatee Lady Young
K poem written about him
K daughter born

1773
2 concerts
London concert with Bach, Eichner, Fischer, Galli, Grassi, Punto, Spandau, Weiss
Blandford concert
K organized concerts
K given annuity of £50 from Thomas Anson

1774
5 concerts
London concert with Bach, Beer, Cramer, Crosdill, Fischer, Grassi, Parke, Ritter, Weiss
Blandford concert
Salisbury concert 2x
1 publication
K organized concerts

1775
4 concerts
London concert with Bach 2x, Bonapace, Cervetto 2x, Clementi, Corri, Cramer, Crosdill, Fischer 3x, Jameson, Jones, Tacet 2x, Weichsell
Newberry concert?
Salisbury concert
9 publications

Dedicatee: Miss Ottley, Richard Ottley, Countess Spencer, Newberry
Assembly
K organized concerts
K son born

1776
2 concerts
London concert with Bach, Cervetto, Cramer, Crosdill, Fischer, Giardini, Grassi, Savoi
Salisbury concert
2 publications
Dedicatee: Duke of Devonshire

1777
2 concerts
London concert with balcony 2x, Cramer, Crosdill 2x, Fischer 2x, Florio, Giardini, Massimino, Tenduucci, Vachon, Weiss
K son born
K given £200 by Thomas Stanton

1778
3 concerts
London concert with Amantini, Bach 2x, Balconi, Cramer 2x, Crosdill 3x, Edicatt, Fischer 2x, Florio, Lidl, Stamitz 2x, Tenducci
Winchester concert
1 publication
Dedicatee Lady Banks
K – given £200 by John Hoper

1779
4 concerts
London concert with Bach, Cramer, Crosdill 3x, Decamp, Edicatt 2x, Fischer 3x, Giorgi 2x, Lidl 3x, Tenducci 2x, Weichsel
K son born
K joined Freemasons

1780
1 concert
London concert with Bach, Crosdill, Edicatt, Fischer, Rauzzini, Weiss
9 publications
Dedicatee John Sole, Page Turner, Aylesford, Duke of Dorset
K son born
K given £175 by John Hayward

1781
1 concert
London concert with Ansani, Crosdill, Fischer, Salomon
1 publication
Dedicatee Lady Banks

1782
2 concerts
London concert with Crosdill, Fischer, Jones, Nicolai, Pieltain, Tenducci, Wheeler
Salisbury concert
1 publication

1783
1 publication

1784
1 publication
Dedicatee William Young
K Will
K Kent visit?
K death
Reeve Charles, executor
Besser Charles C., executor
Starling Benjamin, executor
Reeve Thomas, witness
Donaghoe Michael - moved into K's house